I AM WEALTHIER THAN DONALD TRUMP

A World Traveler's Analysis of a Former President

WOLFGANG GOLSER

For the Center for Biological Diversity

The Center for Biological Diversity is world-renowned. It is a non-profit organization that works to protect endangered species, wild places, and global climate. The Center for Biological Diversity recognizes that the welfare of human beings is deeply connected to nature. This includes the existence in our world of vastly diverse wild animals and plants. Biological diversity has intrinsic value, and its loss impoverishes society. The Center works to secure a future for all species, great and small, that hover on the brink of extinction by utilizing science, law, and creative media. Its emphasis is to protect the lands, waters, and climate that species need to survive.

CONTENTS

PREFACE

"This inner severance from the affliction of misery is spirituality.
It should be practiced with determination and with a heart,
which refuses to be depressed."
—Bhagavad Gita 6:23

Much has been on my mind that needs to be expressed. Things in this world are at a crossroads. This is such a bizarre time we are living in—as if a darkness has arisen—but *light* must take form to confront it!

It is important to be myself! What others say should be judged for its intrinsic value. If one has certain convictions, one must remain true to them. In addition, the present is a boundary between the past and the future. Although it is important to plan for the future, it is also important to live in the present. Mindfulness is the key to living in the present.

Referring to the recent past, there have been several deaths in my family, and quite a few friends of mine are no longer with us. Consequently, I may feel more alone. At the same time, I can be the best companion for myself. Many know that I am a world traveler, as I have traveled to some very interesting places, such as Nepal, India, Tibet, and many other countries, where I have become familiar with Eastern philosophies and meditation practices. Meanwhile, I am finding that with quite a few people no longer in my life, I meet other people who are interested in subjects that are similar to my interests. There are times when it is good to be alone. There are also times when it is great to have quality time with friends.

On the other hand, I had coworkers at a job a long time ago whom I could not have any meaningful conversations with. They just wanted to spend their time in bars and nightclubs to drink beer and talk about stupid, senseless, and meaningless nonsense and gossip. These experiences reinforced my need to be with people who enjoy discussing meaningful topics: science, current affairs, history, philosophy, religion, travel, the natural world, and spiritual subject matters. Those former coworkers knew that I practice meditation and that I have taken certain vows of Buddhism. One of those vows is that I abstain from intoxicants. Oh, yes! Those coworkers always found something about me that they wanted to laugh at, including the fact that I refrain from drinking alcoholic beverages. They wanted to laugh at me all the time! Through and despite all of this, I actually found this entertaining because I remembered a quote: "Wer zuletzt lacht, lacht am besten!" (The literal translation into English is "Those who laugh last, laugh best," although I have also heard the expression "Those who laugh first, laugh last!")

I consider myself an intellectual, and my interests include science (physics, astronomy, geosciences, computer science, and various disciplines in the life sciences), history, philosophy (Western and Eastern), psychology, and religion.

Having traveled to so many countries, I have seen much of the natural world and its various cultures. I am incorporating my travel experiences into my writing. While I was traveling through many Asian countries, it became clear to me how learning is a two-way street: I am learning from others, and others are learning from me. When I did a thirteen-day trek in the Himalayas (the Annapurna Himal), backpacking from village to village, I was traveling with a guide whom I hired out of Kathmandu. He was able to set up an interview with the head lama of a Tibetan Buddhist monastery outside of Pokhara. This allowed me to ask questions about Buddhism, meditation practice, religion, and the difficulties that the Tibetan people encounter. Since that day, I have been diligently and ardently practicing meditation.

My travels and meditation practice have set me on a journey that is beyond what I could have ever imagined.

INTRODUCTION

*"All things are connected.
Whatever befalls the earth, befalls the children of the earth."*
—Chief Seattle, leader of the Suquamish and Duwamish peoples

Constantly, I ask myself, "What kind of a world are we living in?" We seem to live in a world where there is so much strife, tension, and conflict. Everywhere around the world, there is such animosity among people that what seems to have been glowing embers in the past has developed into the raging fires of warfare and conflict. This is especially true in the Middle East.

In addition, I feel that our education system has failed so many people. Many simply do not know what they should know. This goes hand in hand with an anti-intellectual attitude or demeanor in our society.

I feel that my writing can influence a great sector of the general public. There is a good portion of the world that is already on board. They have a good or reasonably good comprehension of the state of affairs of our world. There is a second segment of society that may understand something on a more unconscious level, when something has partially filtered into their minds. They see bits and pieces but have not put it all together yet. There is a third segment of society that may be unaware because they have allowed themselves to be complacent and even deluded. There is a dumbing down in the United States and elsewhere. This is very evident in a slow decay of substantive content in the enormously influential media and television programming that crosses the entire political spectrum.

Within the United States, the political situation is extremely polarized. The people who regard themselves as conservative make a lot of noise. The people who regard themselves as liberal also make a lot of noise. The US Congress is often gridlocked in its legislative activities. Civil discourse has eroded, and acrimony frequently prevails.

Enter Donald Trump!

Chapter 1

WHO IS DONALD TRUMP?

"Growth for the sake of growth is the ideology of the cancer cell."
—Edward Abbey, 1927–1989

To start off, Donald Trump was a very controversial figure in the United States as he became its forty-fifth president. He entered a political arena that had already been highly politically charged and introduced more political acrimony and divisiveness. Perhaps he is a symptom of the problems, yet he has become the cause of more problems.

As a result of the previous presidential administrations, a large segment of the population demanded a change from the usual manner in which politics is conducted. This is the political environment Donald Trump, a billionaire real-estate mogul and former reality-television personality, entered when he took office as the president of the United States on January 20, 2017, by Chief Justice of the United States John Roberts. Trump took the oath of office placing his hand on the Bible that was used at Abraham Lincoln's inauguration and his own family Bible. (That Bible was presented to him by his mother in 1955 when he graduated from Sunday school at his family's Presbyterian church.).

Donald Trump was born on June 14, 1946, in Queens, New

York.[1] Donald was the fourth of five children, and his parents were Frederick C. and Mary Anne MacLeod Trump.[2] His father, Frederick Trump, was a builder and real-estate developer who specialized in the construction and operations of middle-income apartments in Queens, Staten Island, and Brooklyn. His mother immigrated from Tong, Scotland, in 1929 at the age of seventeen. She married Fred Trump in 1936, and the couple settled in Jamaica, Queens, a neighborhood that was, at that time, filled with Western European immigrants.[3] Donald Trump was raised Presbyterian by his mother. He has identified himself as a mainline Protestant.[4]

Trump started his education at Kew-Forest School from kindergarten through seventh grade. He was an assertive and energetic child; therefore, his parents sent him to the New York Military Academy at age thirteen.[5] The intent was to allow the discipline of the school to channel his energy in a positive manner. Trump did quite well at the academy, socially and academically. He rose to become an athlete and student leader by the time he graduated in 1964.

He entered Fordham University. Two years later, he transferred to the Wharton School of Finance at the University of Pennsylvania.[6] He graduated in 1968 with a degree in economics. During his years at college, Trump worked at his father's real-estate business during the summer. Donald Trump was strongly influenced by his father in his decision to pursue a career in real-estate development; however, his personal goals were much grander than those of his father.[7]

After graduating from college, Trump joined the family business, E. Trump and Son, renamed by Trump to the Trump Organization.[8] In 1971, Trump moved his residence to Manhattan, where he became familiar with many influential people. Convinced of the economic opportunity in the city, Trump became involved in several large building projects in Manhattan. They offered opportunities to earn high profits, utilized attractive architectural design, and won public recognition. For example, in 1980, he opened the Grand Hyatt New York, which made him the city's best-known developer.[9]

In 1977, Trump married his first wife, Ivana Zelnickova Winklmayr.[10] She was a New York fashion model who had been an alternate on the 1972 Czech Olympic Ski Team.[11] After the 1977 birth of the couple's first of three children, Donald John Trump Jr., Ivana Trump was named vice president in charge of design in the Trump Organization. She played a major role in supervising the renovation of the Commodore and the Plaza Hotels. It was in 1988 that he acquired the Plaza Hotel for $407 million and spent $50 million renovating it under her direction.[12] The couple had two more children together, Ivanka Trump (born in 1981) and Eric Trump (born in 1984). The Trumps subsequently went through a highly publicized divorce, which was finalized in 1992.[13]

In 1979, Trump rented a site on Fifth Avenue next to the famous Tiffany & Company. This was the location for a monumental $200 million apartment-retail complex designed by Der Scutt. It was named Trump Tower when it opened in 1982.[14] The fifty-eight-story building featured a six-story courtyard lined with pink marble and included an eighty-foot waterfall. The luxurious building attracted well-known retail stores and celebrity renters and brought Trump national attention.

Meanwhile, Donald Trump was investigating the profitable casino gambling business. Casino gambling became legal in New Jersey in 1977. In 1980, Trump acquired a piece of property in Atlantic City, New Jersey.[15] He brought in his younger brother Robert to head up the complex project of acquiring the land, winning a gambling license, and obtaining permits and financing. Holiday Inn Corporation, the parent company of Harrah's casino hotels, offered a partnership, and the $250 million complex opened in 1982 as Harrah's at Trump Plaza. Trump bought out Holiday Inn in 1986 and renamed the facility Trump Plaza Hotel and Casino.[16] Trump also purchased a Hilton Hotels casino hotel in Atlantic City. When the corporation failed to obtain a gambling license, the $320 million complex was renamed Trump's Castle. Later, while it was under construction, he was able to acquire the largest casino hotel in the world at that time, the Taj Mahal in Atlantic City, which opened in 1990.[17]

In New York City, Trump purchased an apartment building, the Barbizon-Plaza Hotel, and 100 Central Park South, which faced Central Park, from Banque Lambert in 1981 for $65 million. This purchase was financed by a $50 million loan from Chase Manhattan Bank.[18] He had plans to build a large condominium tower on the site; however, the tenants of the apartment building were protected by the city's rent control and rent stabilization programs. Those tenants fought Trump's plans and won. Trump then renovated the Barbizon, renaming it Trump Park.[19]

In 1985, Trump purchased seventy-six acres on the west side of Manhattan for $88 million on which he planned to construct a complex called Television City. This was to consist of a dozen skyscrapers, a mall, and a riverfront park. The huge development was to stress television production and feature the world's tallest building; however, community opposition and a long city-approval process delayed construction of the project.[20]

It was in 1990, however, that the real-estate market declined when the US economy fell into recession. Many of Trump's businesses suffered, reducing the value of and income from Trump's empire, and he soon had trouble making payments on his approximately $5 billion debt, some $900 million of which he had personally guaranteed. His own net worth plummeted from an estimated $1.7 billion to $500 million. The Trump Organization required massive loans to keep it from collapsing. Under a restructuring agreement with several banks, Trump was forced to surrender his airline, which was taken over by US Airways in 1992; to sell the *Trump Princess*; to take out second or third mortgages on nearly all of his properties and reduce his ownership stakes in them; and to commit himself to living on a personal budget of $450 thousand a year. This situation raised questions as to whether the corporation could survive bankruptcy.[21] The Trump Taj Mahal declared bankruptcy in 1991, and two other casinos owned by Trump, as well as his Plaza Hotel in New York City, went bankrupt in 1992. Following those setbacks, most major banks refused to do any further business with him.[22]

Trump's fortunes rebounded with the stronger economy of the later 1990s and with the decision of the Frankfurt-based Deutsche Bank AG to establish a presence in the US commercial real-estate market. Deutsche Bank extended hundreds of millions of dollars in credit to Trump in the late 1990s and the 2000s for projects including Trump World Tower (2001) in New York and Trump International Hotel and Tower (2009) in Chicago. In the early 1990s, Trump had floated a plan to his creditors to convert his Mar-a-Lago estate into a luxury housing development consisting of several smaller mansions, but local opposition led him instead to turn it into a private club, which was opened in 1995.[23] In 1996, Trump partnered with the NBC television network to purchase the Miss Universe Organization, which produced the Miss Universe, Miss USA, and Miss Teen USA beauty pageants.[24] Trump's casino businesses continued to struggle, however. In 2004, his company Trump Hotels & Casino Resorts filed for bankruptcy after several of its properties accumulated unmanageable debt, and the same company, renamed Trump Entertainment Resorts, went bankrupt again in 2009.[25]

Trump also coauthored a number of books on entrepreneurship and his business career, including *Trump: The Art of the Deal*

(1987), *Trump: The Art of the Comeback* (1997), *Why We Want You to Be Rich* (2006), *Trump 101: The Way to Success* (2006), and *Trump Never Give Up: How I Turned My Biggest Challenges into Success* (2008).[26] Many of his books were ghostwritten.[27]

Trump marketed his name as a brand in numerous business ventures, including Trump Financial, a mortgage company, and the Trump Entrepreneur Initiative (formerly Trump University), which was an online education company that focused on real-estate investment and entrepreneurship.[28]

Some observers saw Trump's decline as symbolic of many of the business, economic, and social excesses from the 1980s. However, Trump climbed back and was reported to be worth close to $2 billion in 1997. Also, Donald Trump's image was tarnished by the publicity surrounding his controversial separation and later divorce from his wife, Ivana. But Trump married again, this time to Marla Maples, a fledgling actress. The couple had a daughter two months before their marriage in 1993. He filed for a highly publicized divorce from Maples in 1997, which became final in June 1999.[29] His father, Fred, died in 1999, and his mother, Mary, passed away the following year.

Mary Trump is the daughter of the older brother of Donald, Frederick Trump Jr. She is cognizant of what was happening behind the scenes of the Trump business operations, which were based upon easy money, glitz, and glamor. The casinos were business opportunities, which Trump could pursue beyond his father's purview. That appealed to him, as the casino is an environment where the house always wins. Operating a casino required setting aside massive monetary investments and maintaining an ongoing business. The Grand Hyatt and Trump Tower were development projects, which served as a springboard for him to succeed independently of his father. Furthermore, having a casino would serve as his canvas that would allow him to shape his world to his liking.

No doubt, if having one casino was not sufficient, would not two or three be better? One casino might be a cash cow; however, would three become a herd? Of course, operating casinos is not the same as owning and running rental properties in Brooklyn. This was something that Trump did *not* understand. It was inevitable that his casinos would compete with one another and eventually would be cannibalizing one another's profits. Trump never made the distinction between the business models of managing rental properties and running casinos. This, in turn, led to the resulting scenario in which the banks and investors in his first two casinos did not express any objections with greater concern when he intended to open his third casino. If someone had examined the math—even casually—it would have been determined that such investments would not be profitable. This should have scared away even the most foolhardy investors and lenders. That was the 1980s when nobody said no to Donald Trump, resulting in providing legitimacy to his projects that were completely misguided. These were the scenarios that only served to bolster and fuel Trump's ego, along with his delusions of grandeur.[30]

Trump began his political career on October 7, 1999, as he announced the formation of an exploratory committee to inform his decision of whether or not he should seek the Reform Party's nomination for the presidential race of 2000; however, he backed out because of problems within that political party.[31]

In 2004, in addition to his real-estate ventures, Trump premiered a reality television series, *The Apprentice*, which featured contestants competing in various challenges to become one of his employees.[32] The Emmy-nominated show, in which Trump starred, popularized the phrase "You're fired!" and helped him to promote his reputation as a shrewd businessman. In 2008, the show was revamped as *The Celebrity Apprentice* with news makers and entertainers as contestants.[33]

He again publicly announced he would be running for president in the 2012 election, but he withdrew again. He did, however, maintain a high public profile during the election.[34] In 2015, Trump once again turned his attention to politics and announced his candidacy for president of the United States on the Republican ticket.[35]

Trump quickly established himself as a political outsider, a stance that proved popular with many voters—especially those in the Tea Party movement—and he frequently topped opinion polls, besting established Republican politicians.[36] However, his campaign was often mired in controversy, much of it of his own making. In speeches and especially via Twitter (now X), a social medium he used frequently, Trump regularly made inflammatory remarks, including some that were interpreted as racist or sexist. Other public comments by Trump, especially those directed at his rivals or detractors in the Republican establishment, were widely criticized for their unusual belligerence, their bullying tone, and their indulgence in crude personal insults. Trump's initial refusal to condemn the Ku Klux Klan after a former Klansman endorsed him also drew sharp criticism, as did his failure to repudiate racist elements among his supporters in the "alt-right" movement (a loose association of self-described white nationalists, far-right libertarians, and Neo-Nazis).[37] While Trump's comments worried the Republican establishment, his supporters were pleased by his combativeness and his apparent willingness to say whatever came into his mind, a sign of honesty and courage in their estimation. After a loss in the Iowa caucuses to open the primary season in February 2016, Trump rebounded by winning the next three contests, and he extended his lead with a strong showing on Super Tuesday, when primaries and caucuses were held in eleven states in early March. After a landslide victory in the Indiana primary in May, Trump became the presumptive Republican nominee as his last two opponents, Ted Cruz and John Kasich, dropped out of the race.

It wasn't until the 2016 election that Trump became the official Republican nominee for president. On July 21, 2016, Trump accepted the presidential nomination and announced that Indiana Governor Mike Pence would be his vice presidential running mate at the Republican National Convention in Cleveland.[38] In a speech lasting one hour and fifteen minutes, one of the longest in recent history, Trump outlined the issues he would tackle as president, including violence in America, the economy, immigration, trade, terrorism, and the appointment of Supreme Court justices. He and other speakers harshly criticized the presumptive Democratic nominee, former Secretary of State Hillary Clinton, blaming her for the 2012 attack on the US consulate in Benghazi, Libya, and for allegedly having mishandled classified State Department emails by using a private email server. (Earlier in July, the FBI announced that an investigation of Clinton's use of email as secretary of state had determined that her actions had been "extremely careless" but not criminal.)[39] Trump continued his criticisms of Clinton in the following weeks, routinely referring to her as "Crooked Hillary" and repeatedly vowing to put her in jail if he were elected. Trump's threat to jail his political opponent was unprecedented in modern US political history and was not founded in any constitutional power that a US president would have.

Despite having pledged in 2015 that he would release his tax returns, as every presidential nominee of a major party had done since the 1970s, Trump later changed his mind, explaining that he was under routine audit by the Internal Revenue Service (IRS), though there was no legal bar to releasing his returns under audit, as President Richard Nixon had done in 1973. In January 2017, soon after Trump's inauguration as president, a senior White

House official announced that Trump had no intention of releasing his returns.[40]

Despite his ongoing efforts to portray Clinton as "crooked" and an "insider," Trump trailed her in almost all polls. As election day neared, he repeatedly claimed that the election was "rigged" and that the press was treating him unfairly by reporting "fake news," a term he used frequently to disparage news reports that contained negative information about him. He received no endorsements from major newspapers. During the third and final presidential debate in October 2016, he made headlines when he refused to say that he would accept the election results. Although Trump won the electoral college vote by 304 to 227 and thereby the presidency, he lost the nationwide popular vote by more than 2.8 million.[41] (After the election, Trump repeatedly claimed, without evidence, that three to five million people had voted for Clinton illegally.)

Trump's unexpected victory prompted much discussion in the press regarding the reliability of polls and the strategic mistakes of the Clinton campaign. Most analysts agreed that Clinton had taken for granted some of her core constituencies (such as women and minorities) and that Trump had effectively capitalized upon the economic anxieties and resentment of working-class whites, particularly men.[42]

As of this writing, Donald Trump is married to Slovenian model Melania Knauss (now Trump), over twenty-three years his junior. In January 2005, the couple married in a highly publicized and lavish wedding. Among the many celebrity guests at the wedding were Hillary Clinton and former President Bill Clinton. Melania gave birth to the Trumps' son, Barron William Trump, in March 2006.[43]

Trump's sons Donald Jr. and Eric worked as executive vice presidents at that time for the Trump Organization and took over the family business while their father served as president. Trump's daughter Ivanka was also an executive vice president of the Trump Organization, but she left the business and her own fashion label to join her father's administration as an unpaid assistant to the president. Her husband, Jared Kushner, was also a senior adviser to President Trump.[44]

Throughout the election, Trump vehemently denied allegations that he had a relationship with Russian President Vladimir Putin and was tied to the hacking of the Democratic National Committee (DNC) emails. In January 2017, a US intelligence report prepared by the Central Intelligence Agency (CIA), Federal Bureau of Investigation (FBI), and National Security Agency (NSA) concluded that Putin had ordered a campaign to influence the US election.[45] "Russia's goals were to undermine public faith in the US democratic process, denigrate Secretary Clinton, and harm her electability and potential presidency. We further assess Putin and the Russian Government developed a clear preference for President-elect Trump," the report said.[46] In my opinion, Vladimir Putin, who is a former KGB (the Soviet Union's State Security Committee) agent, is a criminal and a huckster.

Prior to the release of the report, President-elect Trump had cast doubt on Russian interference and the intelligence community's assessment. Trump received an intelligence briefing on the matter, and in his first press conference as president-elect on January 11, 2017, he acknowledged Russia's interference.[47] However, in subsequent comments, he again refused to condemn Russia for such activity, notably saying on multiple occasions that he believed Putin's denials, as if it were sufficient to just accept his word.[48]

In March 2018, the Trump administration formally acknowledged the charges by issuing sanctions on nineteen Russians for interference in the 2016 presidential election and alleged cyberattacks. Treasury Secretary Steven Mnuchin delivered the announcement, with the president remaining silent on the matter.[49] In July, days before President Trump was to meet with Putin in Finland, Deputy Attorney General Rod Rosenstein announced additional charges against twelve Russian intelligence officers accused of hacking the DNC and the Clinton campaign.

Mary Trump is the daughter of the older brother of Donald, Frederick Trump Jr., and presented some of her reflections about a month after the election. Unable to focus her attention on anything else, she was watching her Twitter feed. Despite the fact that it was not a surprise to her, she observed the quantity and speed of Trump's inflictions upon the nation. These inflictions consisted of lying about the size of the inauguration, complaining about how he was treated, reversing environmental protections, targeting the Affordable Care Act, and enacting a ban on Muslims, which was overwhelming. It also took Mary back to a time when she was sixteen and Trump was forty-two, witnessing how her father was withering away and dying under the contempt of her grandfather. Trump became the perpetrator of those same cruelties that he had learned from his father, inflicting them on official US policies.

The Trump family created an atmosphere of division and chaos that Donald was swimming in. That division allowed him to thrive and benefit. Obviously, it was at the expense of everyone else. Just as the divisive atmosphere had worn down Mary's father, it was wearing down the country. Donald remained unchanged, which had the effect of weakening a potential ability to be kind and forgiving. Any concepts of kindness had no meaning to him. In turn, this translated to how his administration was run, where his party had been subsumed by politics of grievance and entitlement. Because of his deficiencies in understanding anything about history, constitutional principles, diplomacy, geopolitics, or any other subject matter, he perceived all the country's alliances, social policies, and economic policies through the lens of money. Trump was never pressed to demonstrate any knowledge about any subject. The US Treasury was treated as if it were his personal piggy bank. The affairs of running the government were regarded in strictly financial terms. Utilizing his available political position of power, he advanced his own interests and those of his family, his cronies, and other sycophants. Despite Trump's being in the midst of plenty, there would never be enough to go around. This was exactly how Mary Trump's grandfather (Trump's father) ran the family.

Donald Trump has been in the public eye most of his life, receiving much attention and coverage for the past fifty years, yet he has been under little if any scrutiny. Very little effort has been made to understand how he became what he is and the reasons for his failures and absence of fitness for office, even though his character attributes have been commented upon and joked about for a long time. Much of this is because he has been sheltered, whereby he has been shielded from his own limitations, resulting in an inability to succeed alone in the world. Despite his failures, Trump has been awarded in ways that are incomprehensible, and honest work was never required of him. In the White House, he was surrounded by a clique of cronies who praised every one of his statements, covered up his criminal practices, and normalized all of that behavior, to the point that many have become numb to the accumulation of all that has been happening. At this present time in history, the stakes are much higher than at previous times. Unlike previous times in his life, Donald Trump's flaws and failings *cannot* be ignored. They threaten everyone![50]

Furthermore, Donald Trump has a growing arrogance. Partly, this is a defense mechanism for his feelings of abandonment. It is also an antidote to his lack of self-esteem and provides a protective cover for his deep insecurities. As a consequence, this arrogance has allowed him to keep people at arm's length. In Trump's father's household, the environment was of an unhealthy nature, such that the children were made to feel uncomfortable with expressing or confronting emotions. There was a very narrow range of acceptable human feelings. The only expression of affection for others was merely the handshake, which opened and closed any interactions. Donald's father regarded any closeness to other children or authority figures as being a betrayal of his own authority.

Many people are drawn to Donald Trump because they see in him "displays of confidence," a belief that society's rules don't apply to him, and an exaggerated presentation of self-worth; however, what people perceive as strength is actually arrogance. His expression of "accomplishment" is a false bravado, and his perceived charisma is in reality a very superficial interest in others.[51]

In his inaugural speech on January 20, Trump sent a populist message that he would put the American people above politics. "What truly matters is not which party controls our government, but whether our government is controlled by the people," he said. "January 20, 2017, will be remembered as the day the people became the rulers of this nation again." During his speech, he painted a bleak picture of an America that had failed many of its citizens, describing families trapped in poverty, an ineffective education system, and crime, drugs, and gangs. "This American carnage stops right here and stops right now," he said.

The day after Trump's inauguration, millions of protesters demonstrated across the United States and around the world. The Women's March on Washington drew over half a million people to protest President Trump's stance on a variety of issues ranging from immigration to environmental protection.[52]

Trump took an unusually long time to assemble his cabinet, in part because many of his nominations to positions requiring Senate confirmation were filibustered by Democrats. His cabinet was also unusual in that its members were the least diverse in decades and were by far the richest in US history. Some of Trump's cabinet-level appointments were closely associated with the firms or industries that their agencies were charged with overseeing or were well-known for having opposed their agencies' basic missions in the past.[53] Particularly controversial were Trump's choice for head of the Environmental Protection Agency (EPA), Scott Pruitt, who, as Oklahoma attorney general, had spent much of his career suing the EPA on behalf of the oil and gas industry, and Trump's choice for secretary of education, Betsy DeVos, who had frequently expressed contempt for public education while promoting and financially supporting school-voucher legislation and charter and private schools. Steve Bannon, the former head of Breitbart News, an alt-right publishing platform, was appointed chief strategist; however, he left the administration after seven months in August 2017. Trump also gave his son-in-law, Jared Kushner, and his daughter, Ivanka Trump, prominent (though unpaid) roles as senior adviser to the president and assistant to the president, respectively.[54]

During the first eighteen months of his administration, several of Trump's cabinet members were accused of ethics violations, including breaches of travel regulations or anti-lobbying laws, as well as inappropriate use of their agencies' resources.

The first one hundred days of Trump's presidency lasted from January 20, 2017, until April 29, 2017. In his first days of his presidency, President Trump issued a number of back-to-back executive orders.[55] They were an attempt to make good on some of his campaign promises. They included several orders aimed at rolling back policies and regulations that were put into place during the Obama administration. Several of Trump's key policies that were enacted during his first one hundred days in office included his Supreme Court nomination, steps toward building a wall on the

Mexico border, a travel ban to the United States for several predominantly Muslim countries, the first moves to dismantle the Affordable Care Act (Obamacare), and the US withdrawal from the Paris Agreement on climate change.[56]

During one of his campaign speeches, he said, "We are going to build a great border wall to stop illegal immigration, to stop the gangs and the violence, and to stop the drugs from pouring into our communities."[57] He also promised supporters that he would renegotiate trade deals, reduce taxes and government regulations, repeal the Affordable Care Act, defend Second Amendment gun rights, and "rebuild our depleted military," asking the countries the United States is protecting "to pay their fair share."[58]

On January 31, 2017, President Trump nominated Judge Neil Gorsuch to the Supreme Court. The forty-nine-year-old conservative judge was appointed by President George W. Bush to the United States Court of Appeals for the Tenth Circuit in Denver. Judge Gorsuch was educated at Columbia, Harvard, and Oxford. He also clerked for Supreme Justices Byron White and Anthony Kennedy. The nomination came after Merrick Garland, President Obama's nominee to replace the late Antonin Scalia, was denied a confirmation hearing by Senate Republicans.[59]

Gorsuch's legal philosophy was considered to be similar to Justice Scalia's. This choice drew strong praise from the conservative side of the aisle. "Millions of voters said this was the single most important issue for them, when they voted for me for president," President Trump said. "I am a man of my word. Today I am keeping another promise to the American people by nominating Neil Gorsuch to the Supreme Court."[60]

After Gorsuch gave three days of testimony before the Senate Judiciary Committee in March, the Senate convened on April 6, 2017, to advance his nomination. Democrats mostly held firm to deny the sixty votes necessary to proceed, resulting in the first successful partisan filibuster of a Supreme Court nominee; however, Republicans quickly countered with another historic move, invoking the "nuclear option."[61] This would lower the threshold for advancing Supreme Court nominations from sixty votes to a simple majority of fifty. On April 7, Gorsuch was confirmed by the Senate to become the 113th justice of the Supreme Court.

The following year, President Trump had another opportunity to continue the rightward push of the Supreme Court. This originated with the retirement of Justice Kennedy. On July 9, 2018, he nominated Brett Kavanaugh, who had a judicial textualist and originalist philosophy similar to Justice Antonin Scalia's. Democrats vowed to fight the nomination; however, their options remained limited as the minority party.[62]

Trump issued an executive order to build a wall at the United States's border with Mexico. In his first televised interview as president, President Trump said the initial construction of the wall would be funded by US taxpayer dollars. He also said that Mexico would reimburse the United States "100 percent" in a plan to be negotiated and that it might include a suggested import tax on Mexican goods. In response to the new administration's stance on a border wall, Mexican president Enrique Peña Nieto canceled a planned visit to meet with President Trump. The Mexican president said in a video statement, "Mexico does not believe in walls! I've said time and again; Mexico will not pay for any wall!" Trump and Peña Nieto spoke on the phone after their in-person meeting was canceled. With this, they "agreed at this point not to speak publicly about this controversial issue," according to a statement from the Mexican government.[63]

The wall failed to materialize from either Mexico or Congress; therefore, Trump resorted to another plan. In April 2018, he announced that he would reinforce security along the US border with Mexico by using American troops because of the "horrible, unsafe laws" that left the country vulnerable. The following day, the president signed a proclamation that directed National Guard troops to the US-Mexico border.[64]

The Department of Homeland Security said that the deployment would be in coordination with state governors. Those troops would "support federal law enforcement personnel, including Customs and Border Protection," and federal immigration authorities would "direct enforcement efforts." The exact number of troops and duration of deployment had yet to be determined.

One of the areas in which the Trump administration was able to move quickly to implement its policies was the environment because many of the changes it sought could be accomplished through executive action by Trump or his appointees. Other changes were undertaken through legislation adopted by Congress, whose Republican majority generally shared Trump's environmental views.[65]

Trump signed legislation to block an Interior Department rule that would have restricted the dumping of toxic mining waste into streams and other waterways. EPA administrator Pruitt withdrew an EPA request that oil and natural gas companies report methane emissions from their facilities and rejected a total ban on the pesticide chlorpyrifos against the advice of the EPA's own scientists. Other significant decisions included drastically reducing the size of national monuments created by Obama and President Bill Clinton.[66]

Undoubtedly the most momentous environmental decision of the new Trump administration was Trump's announcement in June that the United States would withdraw from the Paris Agreement on climate change, under which the United States and 194 other countries had agreed to a broad range of measures intended to limit potentially catastrophic increases in global average temperatures during the twenty-first century and to mitigate the economic consequences of global warming.[67] Trump contended that the agreement would harm the American economy (through government-mandated reductions in the country's greenhouse-gas emissions) and was in other respects unfair and even demeaning to the United States—historically the largest emitter of greenhouse gases and, in the early twenty-first century, the second largest emitter after China. Trump's decision was condemned by government and political leaders, scientists, business executives, and activists throughout the world; however, it was praised by Republicans in Congress, who viewed it as a reassertion of American independence in world affairs and a repudiation of the environmental policies of the Obama administration.[68] Like Trump, many Republican lawmakers doubted that climate change was real, while others questioned the human origins of global warming.

A major theme of Trump's presidential campaign was his view that the United States had long been treated unfairly or taken advantage of by other countries, including by some traditional US allies, and that under Obama's leadership the United States had ceased to be respected in world affairs. In numerous speeches, tweets, and interviews, he threatened to impose tariffs on countries that engaged in what he deemed unfair trade practices; harshly criticized the World Trade Organization (WTO); and promised to renegotiate the North American Free Trade Agreement (NAFTA), which he called "the worst trade deal" the United States had ever signed. He also criticized the North Atlantic Treaty Organization (NATO), dismissing the alliance as "obsolete" but also insisting that other NATO countries devote more of their budgets to defense spending. In January 2017, he withdrew the United States from the Trans-Pacific Partnership, a regional trade agreement between twelve Pacific Rim countries that had been a major foreign policy achievement of the Obama administration. (Trump's action was largely symbolic, however, because Congress had never ratified the treaty.)

Trump's personal style was unusual, if not unique, among national political figures in modern US history. This was in part a reflection of his experiences as a prominent figure in the New York real-estate industry; Trump was fiercely competitive as well as intensely concerned with demonstrating his success and accomplishments to others. Indeed, from the very beginning of his career, he cultivated and cherished his reputation as a shrewd businessman, an image that often aided him in his real-estate dealings and which he eventually exploited as a brand beginning in the 1990s. That concern, however, was accompanied by an unusual sensitivity to criticism and a tendency to retaliate harshly against those who he believed had betrayed him or had treated him unfairly. His longtime mentor, friend, and legal adviser Roy Cohn (who had assisted Joseph McCarthy's investigations of alleged communist subversion in the US government in the 1950s) had encouraged him in the latter regard, counseling him on numerous occasions never to apologize (because it is a sign of weakness) and always to hit back harder than you are hit, as Trump put the lesson in *The Art of the Deal*. As he declared in a tweet in 2012, "When someone attacks me, I always attack back…except 100x more. This has nothing to do with a tirade but rather, a way of life!"

In keeping with his bellicose and confrontational style, Trump in his business career characteristically used blunt language as a weapon against his rivals and adversaries, pointedly insulting or belittling them in the press in retaliation for their real or perceived slights. Perhaps surprisingly, Trump did not significantly alter his style or temper his rhetoric upon his entry into politics, notwithstanding the conventional view that success in politics is necessarily a matter of persuasion and compromise rather than "hitting back harder." The advent of Twitter in 2006 eventually gave Trump (who joined the service in 2009) a larger platform for his unfiltered political comments, and he began to regularly tweet about politics in about 2011. During the presidential primaries and in the 2015–16 election campaign, Trump frequently used his Twitter account, which had more than forty million followers, to angrily attack Democrats, his Republican rivals and critics, the news media, job-exporting corporations, and anyone else who had provoked his ire in comments that were widely perceived as aggressive, boastful, petty, and vulgar.[69] Trump similarly declined to filter himself in speeches. This included even mocking the disability of a reporter he disliked. Another unique feature of Trump's rhetoric was the large number of his public statements that were shown by the press or by independent fact-checking organizations to be false or misleading. Although critics, including some in the Republican Party, occasionally admonished him for what they considered undignified behavior, their condemnation only provoked him to fresh attacks. Despite some speculation after his election that the weight of the presidential office and his eventual need for tangible political and diplomatic successes would lead him to adopt a more conventional demeanor, his confrontational style and rhetoric continued unchanged through the first year of his presidency, and indeed the targets of his attacks only expanded. This certainly included his perceived enemies in the FBI and the Justice Department as well as National Football League (NFL) players, who had protested police brutality by kneeling during the playing of the national anthem at football games. In any event, Trump certainly distinguished himself from previous US presidents by his heavy use of social media. He was the first president to rely on Twitter as a primary means of communication with his political supporters and the press, using it even as a venue for semiofficial presidential statements.[70]

Mary Trump stated that Donald's fundamental nature had not

changed. During his presidency, the amount of stress he was under was not attributed to his job. (Donald Trump treated watching TV and tweeting insults as part of the job.) The stress was associated with an effort to keep the public distracted from the fact that he knew nothing. To learn about politics and civics requires work, which he did not want to do. Expressing simple human decency is something that would have required great effort on his part. Trump had been the recipient of good and bad publicity for many decades; however, he had never been subjected to close scrutiny. Also, he had never faced serious opposition. Now, he was being forced to question himself and the world. Because of his maneuvering to solve his problems and his attempts to pretend that they did not exist, his problems were increasing. Was he prepared to solve his problems? Could he adequately cover his tracks? I doubt it, as he became embroiled in the criminal indictments against him. Some examples are the January 6, 2021, insurrection cae, the classified documents case, and the business falsification records trial! This was because the family system that he was in protected him from his own weaknesses. He never truly learned how to negotiate the wider world.

Those well-guarded padded walls of his family system were beginning to reveal signs of disintegration. The people by whom he was surrounded were more craven but weaker and just as desperate. Their futures and his were directly intertwined, based upon his success and favor. He had a clique of people that would protect him from his own inadequacies, and they failed to see that their own fates would have the same results as others who had pledged any loyalty to him in the past. It was people holding greater power than him who had put him into his position of power; now, it was people of lesser power who were keeping him there.[71]

Trump's rhetoric also raised serious concerns among members of both parties about its potential damage to Americans' respect for democratic institutions, particularly freedom of the press and the rule of law. From early in his presidential campaign, Trump attacked unfavorable press reports about him as "fake news," implying that the news organizations in question knowingly published falsehoods. After his election, Trump frequently condemned most major news organizations as "the enemy of the American people," a phrase reminiscent of totalitarian societies. The effect of his accusations was to engender among his supporters a distrust of and hostility toward major media outlets other than Fox News, which generally supported Trump in its reporting and which he regularly watched. Many political scientists and media scholars also pointed to more general problems, claiming that Trump's efforts to portray the press as untrustworthy had created broad confusion and uncertainty among the electorate about what was true. They also worried that Trump's rhetoric would so diminish public confidence in the press that it would cease to serve effectively as a check on governmental power, the role that the founders of the country had envisioned for it. Analogous concerns were raised about Trump's attacks on individual judges who had issued rulings he disliked and on FBI and Justice Department officials who had participated in the Russia investigation. Here, I am referring to the FBI's probe into connections between Russia and Donald Trump's 2016 presidential campaign.[72] Such rhetoric, it was alleged, encouraged a distorted perception of the judiciary and law-enforcement agencies as inherently biased. Some independent observers, however, regarded those criticisms as overblown, while Trump and his supporters dismissed them as motivated by political bias or by the resentment of Democrats at having lost the presidential election.

Mary Trump presents her point of view of having privilege and neglect simultaneously. Mary Trump felt that she had the material things that she needed. This included private schools and summer camp. There was, however, a built-in idea that it would not last.

Also, there was a dispiriting and devastating sense that whatever anyone did, did not matter. Worse, they did not matter. Only Donald mattered.[73]

What is interesting is that this reflects the current time we live in. Ours is a materialistic society, based upon consumerism. Having had Donald Trump in power is a reflection of that collective materialism. Concurrently, our society is wanting or lacking in so many other ways.

Trump is ignorant of a vast array of issues about which one expects the president of the United States to be at least somewhat literate. That is clearly the case with him. When questions are presented to him that he does not comprehend, the tactic that he resorts to is deception. Trump has an illusion that he has accomplished everything on his own merits. In reality, he has cheated. He has given interviews where he stated that he was loaned about a million dollars, but he claims that he was solely responsible for his success. Is it easy to believe? For many, yes! Unfortunately, he has failed consistently and spectacularly as the ostensible leader of the free world, which is shrinking.

As far as some of his attributes are concerned, he is incapable of growing, he is not able to learn, he can't evolve, he can't regulate his emotions, and he lacks an ability to moderate his responses. Really bad, he is extremely inept at taking in and synthesizing information. Basically, he remains arrested at the mental age of a three-year-old.

Trump has a craving for affirmation that is so great that he is unaware that his greatest supporters are those people whom he would not condescend to be with outside of his rallies. He has deep-seated insecurities that have created within him a need as great as a black hole. He requires the "shining light" of compliments that disappear as soon as he has soaked them all in.

In the case of Donald Trump, this goes beyond the garden variety form of narcissism. Nothing is ever enough with him. Mary

Trump stated her viewpoint very eloquently: "In addition to being weak, he has an extremely fragile ego that has to be bolstered at every moment. Deep down, he knows that he is not at all what he claims to be. This also includes knowing that he has never been loved."[74] He has to draw others in by getting them to assent to the most insignificant thing, such as "Isn't this plane great?" "Yes, Donald, this plane is great." Failing to present him with this small concession is regarded by Trump as an act of rudeness. He makes his vulnerabilities and insecurities other people's responsibility. Others' failing to assuage those insecurities and not taking care of him are things that are unbearable for him. This insecurities leave a big vacuum within him. Those who desire his approval will say anything to obtain it. His perception is that he has suffered immensely; therefore, anyone not alleviating that suffering must also suffer.[75]

As indicated above, Donald Trump had a brother who was eight years older, named Frederick Trump Jr. Their father was an authoritarian workaholic. Similar traits—maybe to a lesser degree—were passed on to Donald Trump. As a child, Fred Jr. wanted to become a pilot; therefore, he went on to study flying. Fred Jr. was listed in newspapers as vice president for E. Trump & Son; however, he had a difficult time working with his father. Consequently, Fred Jr. left his father's company to pursue his dream of being a pilot, quickly being accepted at Trans World Airlines, which created tension with his father. Such differences in the family put pressure on Fred Jr., which might have been the cause of his alcoholism.[76] As a result, Fred Jr. died at the young age of forty-two in 1981. (He was born October 14, 1938, and died Spetember 26, 1981.[77])

Mary Trump provides some insight as to how Fred Jr. was treated. Basically, Trump witnessed his brother's destruction, which was a process lasting forty-two years. The foundation for that was laid early, with the effect on Trump being that he lives in a dark space between fear of indifference and feal of failure. It is failure that led to his brother's destruction as Donald Trump was experiencing his own trauma. The combination of what he witnessed and what he experienced isolated him and terrified him. The fear from Trump's childhood and his present fears can't be overstated, as they originated in the hell that existed in the home six decades ago. Every time one hears Trump talk about how great something is (the best, the biggest, the most tremendous), it is implied that Trump himself was the cause that made it happen. One must remember that when he speaks, it is this little boy that is desperately worried that he, like his older brother, is inadequate. Inadequacy results in destruction, and that is Trump's fear. His false bravado and bragging is, at a deeper level, just directed at his long-dead father instead of the audience in front of him.

Trump also has a way of presenting blanket statements, such as "I know more about [fill in the blank] than anybody, believe me!" Another iteration is "Nobody knows more about [fill in the blank] than me." With these statements, he rants about nuclear weapons, trade with China, and many other subjects about which he knows absolutely nothing. He has also gone essentially unchallenged when touting the efficacy of drugs that have *not* been tested for the treatment of COVID-19. Lastly, he engages in an absurd revisionist history in which he never makes a mistake and nothing is his fault.[78]

In December 2019, a new coronavirus, COVID-19, erupted in Wuhan, China. The SARS-CoV-2 virus spread worldwide within weeks. The first confirmed case in the United States was reported on January 20, 2020. Trump was slow to address the spread of the disease, initially dismissing the imminent threat and ignoring persistent public health warnings and calls for action from health officials within his administration and Secretary Azar. Instead, throughout January and February, Trump focused on economic and political considerations of the outbreak.[79]

Mary Trump presents criticisms of Trump's slow response to the coronavirus epidemic. Basically, any criticism or rebuke that is presented to Trump is regarded as a challenge, which results in his doubling down on the behavior that drew fire in the first place. Any criticism is a green light to do worse. His father, Fred, appreciated Trump's obstinacy because it signaled the kind of toughness he was seeking in his sons. Unfortunately, fifty years later, people were literally dying of COVID-19, which was the result of his catastrophic decisions and disastrous inaction. With millions of lives at stake, Trump took accusations about the federal government's failure to provide ventilators personally. Then he threatened to withhold funding and lifesaving equipment from states whose governors didn't pay sufficient homage to him. Trump taking things personally is *not* surprising! There was a deafening silence in response from his followers to such a blatant display of sociopathic disregard for human life and the consequences for one's actions. Trump has continually been given a pass and rewarded for his failures and for his transgressions—against tradition, against decency, against the law, and against fellow human beings. His acquittal in the Senate impeachment trial was another such reward for bad behavior.

Despite the fact that lies are true in Trump's mind, they are still lies. He just wants to see what he can get away with in the end, which, until now, has been everything.[80]

During Trump's initial response to COVID-19, his objective was to minimize negativity at all costs. Fear—the equivalent of weakness in his family—was as unacceptable to him now as it was when he was three years old. When Trump is in the deepest trouble, there are no superlatives available to describe the situation. The situations and his responses to them must be unique—even if absurd or nonsensical. On his watch, has any hurricane ever been as wet as Hurricane Maria? "Nobody could have predicted" a pandemic that his own Department of Health and Human Services was running simulations for just a few months before COVID-19 struck in Washington state. Why does he minimize negativity? Fear!

Why did Trump drag his feet in December 2019 and in January, February, and March 2020? He only did it because of his fear of appearing weak. He wanted to project a message that everything was "great," "beautiful," and "perfect." Here, the irony is that his failure to face the truth resulted in massive failure anyway. The lives of over a million people were lost. Also, the economy of the richest country in history could have been destroyed. Trump will never acknowledge any of this. He will move the goalposts to hide any evidence and convince himself in the process that he did a better job than anybody else could have done—if only a few hundred thousand die instead of two million!

"Get even with people who have screwed you" is one of Trump's greatest quotes; however, often the person he's getting revenge on is somebody he has screwed over first, such as the contractors that he refused to pay or the niece and nephew he refused to protect. Even when he manages to hit his target, his aim is extremely bad. This results in lots of collateral damage. Andrew Cuomo, who was the governor of New York and the de facto leader of the country's COVID-19 response during his time as governor, committed the sin of insufficiently kissing Trump's ass. He committed the ultimate sin of showing Trump that he was better and more competent, a real leader under those circumstances who was respected, effective, and admired. Trump was not able to fight back by shutting Cuomo up or reversing his decisions. As Trump abdicated his authority to lead a nationwide response, he did not have the ability to counter decisions made at the state level. Trump insulted Cuomo and complained about him; however, as the days passed, it became clear that Trump was petty, pathetic, ignorant, and delusional in how he handled the COVID-19 pandemic. What Trump did in order to offset the powerlessness and rage he felt was to punish everyone else. If it suited his agenda, he withheld ventilators or stole supplies from states that had not groveled sufficiently. This created a situation in which Cuomo would look bad if New York did not have enough equipment. The rest of us be damned! Thankfully, Trump didn't have many supporters in New York City; nevertheless, even some of those did die because of his craven need for revenge. What Trump thought was justified retaliation was, in this context, mass murder.[81]

In addition, it is stupefying to witness how everything regarding the coronavirus has become so politicized. Take for example, the wearing of masks! I can make an analogy, regarding the weather. When I hear a weather report informing me that it is going to rain, I will either wear a rain poncho or take my umbrella. Likewise, if I am informed that the coronavirus is spreading, I will wear a face mask. My wearing a rain poncho or taking an umbrella has absolutely *nothing* to do with who is in any political office. Similarly, my wearing a mask has nothing to do with who is in political office. How low have we come that even the wearing of a face mask to protect oneself or to protect others during a dangerous coronavirus pandemic has become a political statement? Despicable! The coronavirus knows no politics, as it kills regardless of the victim's political affiliation.

There is an alliance between Alex Jones, Roger Stone, Mark Levin, and Donald Trump, who represent the extreme political right. It is stupefying to see what they present, and there is the market out there where people feed off that, as if it were candy.

There is a very gullible public out there that just absorbs the Trump agenda because people have lost their ability to set their own agendas or knowledgeably question those in authority. What authority? It can be political authority. Why can't people question the positions of their own party's political platforms and statements? It could be religious authority. Why can't people question the authority of an ecclesiastical system? Why can't people question the statements of those in religious or political authority? If something seems wrong, why can't they speak out?

Chapter 2

A DOWNWARD POLITICAL SPIRAL?

"We are what we think. All that we are arises with our thoughts.
With our thoughts, we make the world."
—Dhammapada 1:1–2

What is the present state of politics in the United States? Presently, it all is very dysfunctional. There are, of course, the major divisions between the Republicans and Democrats. (Some of us prefer to be unaffiliated with any political party as independents.) Then, even within the political parties, there are divisions that may be acrimonious at times. One needs to only look back at the presidential elections of 2016 and 2020. Wow! Even among the Republicans themselves, there were huge loads of unkind and even obnoxious comments spoken. Also, among the Democrats, there can be acrimony between the more centrist and more progressive Democrats. As I was watching the debates of both major political parties at that time, they came across as being very farcical and comical. Is this the state of affairs which people have lowered themselves to?

On January 8, 2011, there was a shootout that occurred in Tucson, Arizona. In the shootout, several people were killed, and many were wounded. One of the congresswomen from Arizona,

Gabby Giffords, was shot in the head, left barely hanging to life.[1] She recovered; however, she was left with a traumatic brain injury that impeded her ability to speak. The sheriff of Pima County, Clarence Dupnik, made a statement about how there is so much vitriol and acrimony being displayed. Of course, many Republicans objected to this statement because Dupnik was a Democrat.[2] He hit the nail on the head since it is very true that the debates among many politicians are very vitriolic and acrimonious.

There are many problems in the United States and all around the world. When it was least needed, for some reason, Donald Trump was elected. During the political primary campaigns, he was very vitriolic in his demeanor toward other Republicans. No doubt, some of the other Republicans behaved no better. Then, during the campaign for the general election, Trump continued the same course of acrimonious comments, both verbal and on Twitter, against Hilary Clinton. Since the 2016 election, the disparaging comments have *not* ceased. We are *all* feeling the effects of this vitriol.

Once again, I am asking the question: Where are we headed?

As the situation is presently in the world in general and the United States in particular, we are at a crossroads. We do have to be concerned about anthropogenic causes of global warming. There is much corporate greed, as it seems that corporations appear to be more concerned about quarterly reviews, annual reports, and investment portfolios. I am *not* saying that this is wrong in itself, as it is part of doing business. Where the problem lies is with any disregard for the environment—globally or locally—human rights situations, and other undesired long-term consequences.

Here I would like to mention that there is a need for government regulations. I am keenly aware that there can be ludicrous and ineffective regulations that can be stifling and even nonsensical. Then there are outmoded regulations that have served their function; however, with the changing times, changing technologies, and changing political situations, there can be a need to make revisions. There is a reason why we require laws, rules, and regulations. It is to provide order and security. If no regulations exist against dumping toxic wastes into a river, lake, or ocean, as an example, then many corporations will not care. We just need to take a look at Love Canal in the state of New York.[3] When a company dispenses its wastes in a careless or inconsiderate manner, it is an injustice to those people who have to live with them in such close proximity. Is this not why we have "cancer clusters"? In addition, the negative effects those wastes have on wildlife must be taken into consideration.

There is an analogy to governmental rules and regulations. We have the freedom to drive a car. Just as any business, whether it is a big corporation or a local mom-and-pop store, has a right to conduct business affairs as is suitable. But driving a car or any other motor vehicle involves responsibility. There are reasons why there are traffic lights and road signs. The person who drives the car is free to drive their vehicle to the destination of their choice; however, those lights and signs regulate the flow of traffic, allowing everyone to have their opportunity to cross an intersection. This, in turn, allows the driver to reach their destination safely. From time to time, circumstances change as road conditions change or construction projects alter traffic conditions; therefore, the signage may need to be changed. Such understanding applies to business as well, where regulations may have to be changed to accommodate changes in political, social, technological, and other conditions. Using this analogy, rules and regulations are similar and different for big rigs and small vehicles. Of course, all vehicles have to follow the same basic traffic rules; however, there are obvious reasons why large trucks may not be permitted in certain areas. Similarly, large corporations and small businesses need to follow certain basic rules; however, a larger corporation is also going to have some different regulations because of the intrinsic nature of its size and type of business. Certainly, regulations will differ for the type of products manufactured, as a corporation in the pharmaceutical industry is different from a corporation manufacturing motor vehicles or a bank or an energy company and so forth.

This leads me to my next point. Why are people so eager to do away with regulation? With the Trump administration, regulations have been rolled back to satisfy certain political constituents. This is especially true with the coal industry. Does this not mean that coal-burning power plants will be free to be more relaxed with the output of their exhausts into the atmosphere? Of course! Some of these companies have even been involved in scandals, such as Massey Energy Company. Massey Energy owned and operated Upper Big Branch Mine, where twenty-nine miners were killed in April 2010.[4] The Mine Safety and Health Administration (MSHA) found that the company's culture of favoring production over safety contributed to flagrant safety violations that caused the coal-dust explosion. On December 6, 2011, MSHA announced a $10,825,368 levy against Massey, the largest monetary penalty imposed by the agency in history. Then I could envision how the industry would vent more sulfur dioxide and nitrous oxide into the atmosphere to reduce their costs of doing business. Unfortunately, this failure to reduce those emmisions is going to "save pennies" for the short-term; however. It is going to cost much more down the road, because of the the health and environmental effects. I will have more to say about anthropogenic causes of global warming, as the coal, gas, and oil industries want to push through their agendas, and they have their "guys" in high places in political office. This is why people who are environmentally conscious must continue to speak out.

Another point that requires attention is that none of the fossil fuels (coal, oil, and gas) are infinite. There is only so much present on the planet. This means that the time to act is *now* to transition from fossil fuels to renewable energy sources. This is where government should be allowed to lend a helping hand in making certain that rules and regulations are current, not outdated, and are based on common sense. Such was not the case under Donald Trump's administration!

There is an observation I have made in meeting several people who are supporters of Donald Trump. One thing that they have in common is their disdain for Hillary Clinton. A few of them told me that they do not like Trump; however, they voted for him because they regard him as the lesser of the two evils. I can empathize with that because, truthfully, I have many misgivings about Hillary Clinton.

I had a discussion with one of the Trump supporters, and he is a religious person. He began talking to me about the book of Revelation in the Bible. He asked me where I get my news information. I mentioned that I watch the *PBS NewsHour* because I do not watch any of the other television stations. Since he started to talk about religion, I told him that I was not interested; however, he switched the conversation to Donald Trump and told me that he supported Trump because he is a Washington outsider.

I have *no* objection to anyone who is a Washington outsider. In fact, I consider it a good thing because many of the career politicians in Washington have become too embedded in Washington politics and the affairs of the special interests that they no longer have the interests of the people at heart. Many have even become hucksters! My problem is that, as much as I would like to see a political outsider run for the presidency of the United States, Donald Trump is—simply—the *wrong* political outsider. Trump is another huckster! I would like to see a political outsider who is not a huckster. Period!

Chapter 3

THE STATE OF AFFAIRS
IN THE WORLD

"Where the army is, prices are high. When prices rise,
the wealth of the people is exhausted!"
—Sun Tzu, *The Art of War*

Back at the end of 2006 and the beginning of 2007, I took a trip to Syria and Jordan. It was the second time that I was in a Middle Eastern country. This was also another educational experience, as it was a continuation of my learning from my prior trip to Egypt in 2001. There were many cultural similarities between Egypt, Syria, and Jordan because they have a religion in common, Islam, and a very long history, which dates back millennia. (At the time of the 2016 presidential election, the United States was only 240 years old.) In addition to Islam, there are Christian and Jewish minorities. There are also many contrasts between those three countries.

One of the things that I noticed in Egypt among the people was a lot of poverty, despite a cultural richness. Underneath, I saw a lot of discontent, and I even had a feeling that something was bound to happen. When people are under such pressure and poverty, the bottle will become uncorked. My intuition told me that, in time, there was going to be a political upheaval.

37

In Syria, the atmosphere seemed completely different, and it was easier for me to travel. As an example, when I ate at restaurants in Damascus, Aleppo, Homs, Hama, and Palmyra, I experienced some outstandingly good customer service. People seemed to be going about their affairs, minding their own business. Things came across as being quite efficient. Our buses between those cities were very timely and reliable in contrast to Egypt. I would not have envisioned anything like what is presently happening today, with Syria being wracked by civil war and even a civil war within a civil war.

When I was in Palmyra, I was able to hike from the citadel to some Roman ruins and visit the Temple of Baal and the Valley of the Tombs. Palmyra has an interesting and rich history, being between the Roman Empire and the Persian Sasanian Empire. It was from there that Queen Xenobia ruled an independent Palmyrene Empire after the Roman emperor Valerian was taken prisoner by the Persians. It was the Roman emperor Aurelian who reconquered Palmyra, adding it as an eastern extremity of the Roman Empire. Today, Palmyra is in ruins because the Islamic State captured Palmyra, and Bashar al-Assad recaptured it from the Islamic State. The Temple of Baal had been completely destroyed by the Islamic State. Many of the Roman ruins themselves are in ruins—that is, no longer standing.

I am always asking myself how this came to be. The path of my own reading, along with reasoning and reflecting on my time spent in Syria, leads me to believe that the answer lies with a destabilized Iraq. George W. Bush, whom I am extremely critical of, invaded Iraq. When Saddam Hussein was removed from power, the various religious and ethnic groups started to assert themselves. It was at that time, when Iraq fell into chaos, that the Sunnis and Shiites were at war with each other. The only part of Iraq that had stability was the northern part, known as Kurdistan. (Personally, I believe that it should be recognized as an independent nation; however, that is another topic of discussion.)

When Bashar al-Assad made the mistake of suppressing a peaceful movement, those elements that were radicalized and were slowly infiltrating across the border between Iraq and Syria were ready and waiting for new opportunities. In other words, the civil war in Iraq expanded and crossed that international boundary to become the civil war in Syria.

The civil war in Iraq started during George W. Bush's administration; however, the civil war in Syria happened during Barack Obama's administration. Naturally, Barack Obama had nothing to do with the start of that civil war in Syria; however, some of Obama's policies were very vague regarding how to deal with the situation. Although Obama had better intentions of wanting to disengage the United States from the Middle East, the situations in Iraq and Syria had their own inertia that could not be altered.

If Barack Obama's policies could be considered vague, the policies of Donald Trump were even vaguer. I have yet to hear about a position that he wanted to take. Regarding Syria, the Iranians and Russians had their hands in the pie by supporting Bashar al-Assad. Meanwhile, Trump seemed to have been opposing Iran, yet he also seemed to be getting cozy with Vladimir Putin of the Russian Federation. Seems convoluted! Doesn't it?

These combined situations, along with the situations in Egypt, Libya, Yemen, and South Sudan, make the problems of this region seem intractable. Because the democratically elected Mohamed Morsi al-Ayyat was overthrown in a coup d'état by Abdel Fattah El-Sisi, Egypt has basically replaced one dictator with another dictator. Of course, Donald Trump has become quite cozy with that dictator, too. Libya remains a basket case. War has become a cancer throughout the Middle East and northern Africa.

Another country in the Middle East that I visited on a trip to the southern part of the continent of Africa is Qatar. Although I have not been to Saudi Arabia, Qatar is very similar, as it is a country ruled by a sheik or emir. The tensions between Saudi Arabia and Iran are very strong. Into this mix is Turkey, such that there is competition between Iran, Saudi Arabia, and Turkey in this region of the world. This means that there is not only the situation between the Sunnis and the Shiites, but also the overlay of these three powers in the region.

Once again, I cannot emphasize enough how vague Donald Trump's policies were in the region, as he seemed to completely lack any understanding of the history of the Middle East. Although George W. Bush's Middle Eastern policies were very clear—he wanted very badly to invade Iraq—there was no clarity from Donald Trump. The situation with Bush was such that those wars were fought for the ambitions of the few—not the security of the many. Once weapons were manufactured to fight wars. Now wars are manufactured to sell weapons.

Donald Trump's policies had a way of changing from week to week—or even when there were different people in the room or office with him. Doesn't this make it seem like we are living in uncertain times? Yes! There was one thing that remained consistent with Trump, which was his relationship with Israel, where he formally relocated the US embassy to Jerusalem. The good thing is that, during his administration, Trump did not get the United States involved in any additional wars, which was basically because he was operating for his own political convenience. If it had been politically convenient, most definitely, he would have started another armed conflict. I envision that he had Iran in his crosshairs.

There comes a time when one must make references to the past. I would like to begin by making a reference back to one of many important trips in my life. This happened when I took a trip around the planet—basically, flying west.

I was on a trip to Asia and Europe. This was my first trip to Asia, which was in 1994. The one important accomplishment of this trip was a trek in the Himalayas. This trek was for thirteen days in the Annapurna Himal. It was an uplifting experience, which involved being tested physically, ascending and descending the magnificent scenic canyons. The vistas were wonderful, such as the Dhaulagiri Himal. Since it was my first time to Nepal, I had to get accustomed to many things, such as climate, topography, and food. Yet it was vital for me to experience this, as I would find out how my life would be enriched in ways that I could not imagine.

The guide whom I hired was very knowledgeable and helpful. We had the opportunity to discuss many things. Doing the trek together, we encountered other travelers and local people. What struck me of interest was the number of Hindu and Buddhist monks that I met.

It was interesting for me, someone who likes to talk, to just refrain from speaking and to experience the opportunity to listen and learn. Hearing about some of the experiences of those people and why they chose that path was fascinating.

Yes! I found the trek inspiring and physically demanding at the same time. What is more essential is that it became part of my own spiritual path. It was important for me to see and meet those people at those times and places, as if it was meant to transpire in this manner.

The thirteenth day was presented as a gift to me because my guide was able to set up an interview with the head lama of the Jangchub Choeling Monastery and Tashi Palkhiel Tibetan Refugee Settlement near Pokhara, Nepal. Inside the Buddhist meditation sanctuary, I saw statues of the Buddha. One was the big statue at the front of the sanctuary, and others were smaller, representing the various moods of the Buddha. There was a ceremony in progress, and I had the opportunity to witness the event, which involved the playing of Tibetan Buddhist singing bowls and horns. Those horns had great length to convey the various tones. This ceremony was significant for me because I was able to see for myself what the monks valued, which was meditation. This monastery was outside of Pokhara as I was concluding the trek.

The best part of the experience was the interview during which the head lama, my guide, and I had some time together., which allowed me to ask questions about Buddhism, meditation, the Tibetan people, and the issues that faced them. Yes! Prior to this point in time, I had read quite a few books about Buddhism in general, Tibetan Buddhism in particular, and meditation practice. For me, it was an intellectual experience; however, it would prove to be something far bigger in that. From that day on, I would continue practicing my meditation techniques, diligently.

Another thing that I took away from this interview experience was that the Buddhist monks were *not* judgmental in any way. In my prior experience with Western religions—primarily a few Christian denominations—I saw how judgmental the participants or devotees, including the clergy, could be. I always regarded their judgments and hypocrisy as nonsense, and I severed myself many years prior from all that dogmatic rubbish.

Far more important than leaving the rubbish behind, as the snake sheds its skin, it was time to grasp firmly onto something new. That, which was most practical, was meditation. It was time for me to take to heart my meditation practice. Prior to that, it had been off-and-on and unstructured. Henceforth, from that time on, it would be daily, and I would be meditating diligently and in a structured manner.

I continued with my trip, traveling through Bangkok and the

other parts of southern Thailand. I was able to take in the sights of the major Buddhist temples, such as Wat Phra Kaew, Benchamabophit, Wat Intharawihan, and Wat Traimit (the Golden Buddha). The monks present were of a different sect of Buddhism than the ones I encountered in Nepal, who were Tibetan Buddhists. The monks of Thailand are of the Theravada school of Buddhism. As it is with the history of any major religion, it was within my ability to understand that divergences would occur.

During this trip, I saw many natural wonders. What was also brought to my attention, since I am a scientist, was that I would see plants in various plant families that are relatives of plants in Europe and the continent of North America. They also included relatives of plants in the Sonoran Desert of the southwest United States and northern Mexico.

Since my first trip to Asia in 1994, I have been to Asia quite a few times. One of those trips involved visiting Beijing, China, and Tibet. On a prior trip to Asia, I was in India and Nepal, where I experienced interfacing with Hindu and Buddhist monks. It was there, after visiting the monks and having an interview with the head lama of the Tibetan Buddhist monastery just outside Pokhara, Nepal, that I had the intention of visiting the heartland of Tibet.

This trip to Tibet began with a flight from Tucson to San Francisco, and we continued on another flight from San Francisco to Beijing, China, arriving in the late afternoon. The next morning was spent at Tiananmen Square, followed by lunch in town. Then, the afternoon was spent in the Forbidden City, which was the center of the Ming Dynasty. That evening, several of us in the group visited the Liyuan Theater for Chinese opera, involving traditional costumes, music, juggling, and acrobatics.

The next morning was spent in the Yonghe Lama Temple, which is a Tibetan-Mongolian temple built by the Manchu Mongols for the Seventh Dalai Lama and his Mongolian disciple

Changkya Rölpé Dorjé. After lunch in town, we left for the Great Wall, stopping at a jade factory on the way. There, I broke away from the group to do a hike on the Great Wall, going up to the fifth tower. The loop took me about fifty-five minutes to complete, and the views were spectacular.

The next day, we took the flight to Tibet via Chengdu. Because there is only one time zone in China, Tibet remains on Beijing time. Thus one arrives rather late, but, because it is five hours west, the sun remains high in the sky until late in the evening.

The drive from the airport to Tsetang follows the banks of the Yarlung Tsangpo (Brahmaputra River) all the way and offers magnificent vistas. On arrival we checked into the Yulong Hotel.

We began the next morning with a visit to the Yambhu Lagang temple, where we offered a smoke ritual and wind horses, which are Tibetan prayer flags, on the ridge behind the temple. This building originally was a castle, purportedly Tibet's first, built sometime between the fourth and second centuries BCE. It was converted into a temple in the mid-seventh century CE, when Emperor Songtsen Gampo—a predecessor of the soul who became the Dalai Lamas—made Buddhism the national religion of his newly established empire and moved his capital from Tsetang to Lhasa. He was the thirty-third king of Tibet's Yarlung Dynasty. The Yambhu Lagang had been created by the first monarch in this dynasty. Some folks rode horses and yaks up the mountain to the temple. Of course, I hiked, and the altitude had no effect on me.

In the afternoon, we visited the Tradruk Temple, one of the twelve inner circle temples built by Songtsen Gampo in the mid-seventh century. (He built 108 throughout his empire as a geomancy method of establishing harmony with nature.) The town was engaged in a one-week practice of the "Om mani padme hum" mantra, so it was filled with laypeople engaged in the practice.

We had the pleasure of being allowed to sit for meditation in the Chapel of the Pearled Chenrezig, a *thangka* of Avalokiteshvara with thousands of pearls sewn into it. It was an uplifting experience! A thangka is a painting created by the Buddhist monks that depict the life of the Buddha, bodhisattvas, other influential Buddhist monks, or religious symbols.

Around sunset, we visited the Sang Ngak Choling Nunnery (Secret Mantra Dharma Hermitage). We sat with the nuns, led by the abbot, where we were offered yak-butter tea. We made offerings to the nuns and requested a ritual for a safe pilgrimage.

The next morning was a bright sunny day, where we took a boat ride across the Yarlung Tsangpo, followed by trucks and tractors to Samye. There we visited the Samye Monastery, which was the first fully qualified monastery to be built in Tibet around the mid-eighth century. We took the bus back to Tsetang.

The next day, we took a long bus ride to Gyantse. On arrival we visited the Kumbum Stupa, which is an architectural and spiritual jewel with seven stories and seventy-seven chapels. Afterward we walked over to Pelkor Chode Monastery, where the monks graciously opened the chapel of the Tantric mahasiddhas for us and allowed us to meditate inside it for half an hour.

We spent the night in the Gyantse Jian Zang Hotel. Although it has a Chinese name, it is owned by a very sweet young Tibetan doctor. Then, we had an early-morning departure from Gyantse to Shigatse to catch the full-moon Saga Dawa event in Tashi Lhunpo. This is the monastery built by the First Dalai Lama in 1447. Here we meditated in the Tantric chapel created by the Tenth Panchen Lama. After the morning visit to the monastery, we checked into the Manasarovar Hotel and went to the nearby Songtsen Gampo Restaurant for lunch.

In the afternoon we visited the Free Market, so called because, in the Communist days, it was the only open market allowed in the city. The ladies in this market bring a new dimension to the meaning of the words "aggressive marketing."

We began the next morning with a hotel rooftop meditation. After breakfast, we all returned to Tashi Lhunpo Monastery for a second visit. This time the monks allowed the leaders of the group to offer devotions in the private chamber of the early Panchen Lama. This was a great honor because it was in this very room that Helena P. Blavatsky received her transmissions from the Eighth Panchen Lama. After lunch we received permission to visit the Tibet Gang-Gyen Carpet Factory and witness firsthand the exquisite nature of these handmade masterpieces.

We experienced an unpleasant incident in the midst of this sacred atmosphere. Initially, our tour leader and organizer usually worked with Tibetan guides. On this occasion, he was told that, with a group this size, he would be assigned certain guides. The reason? There was an incident at Mount Everest (on the Tibet side) in April when a Tibetan went to the peak and placed a "Free Tibet Now" flag. The Chinese authorities were incensed. Although our "security guides" were indeed helpful, friendly, and courteous—especially for those people having a difficult time at the higher altitudes—they played dual roles as tour guides and reporters of the suspicious (in their eyes) activities, including our conversations, of our group of forty-four Westerners. This scrutiny also involved one of them taking pictures of members of our group, as well as native Tibetans and their villages. The tension with the security people reached a peak in Shigatse. There at the Tashi Lhumpo Monastery, a leading monk allowed the several leaders of our group "to offer devotions in the private chamber of the early Panchen Lama." This was a great honor, because we were also told this was the first time in twenty years that white people (or those from the West) had been allowed into the chamber. So our group waited outside for about twenty minutes while these four people went inside the private chamber and spent time with this monk. This angered the Chinese security tour leader because he wasn't able to report on what took place during the time in that room. He immediately got on the phone to his superior to get orders on what to do. Then after about ten minutes passed, he and three other security guides from our group began to push and harass a monk outside the door, trying to force him to get a key or gain entrance to this chamber. There were two people from our group who witnessed this harassment.

The next day after breakfast, we said goodbye to Shigatse and left on an all-day drive to Lhasa with a side visit to the Turquoise Lake. We picnicked beside the lake at some 16,500 feet above sea level. The site offered exquisite views of the Turquoise Lake and surrounding mountain ranges, with glaciers in the background. This is one of the four most sacred lakes in Tibet. We arrived in Lhasa in the late afternoon, and after checking into the Kyichu Hotel, we went for an early evening walk around the Barkhor (Middle Circle) around the Jokhang Temple.

The next day, we took a trip to Drak Yerpa, the cave complex to the east of Lhasa, where Atisha meditated and taught for many years with his principal disciple Lama Drom Tonpa. We did meditation in the cave temple associated with Padmasambhava, the eighth-century Indian master, who built the Samye Monastery. The dozens of caves on this mountain served as meditation places for many of Tibet's greatest masters, including many of the Dalai and Panchen lamas. We hung prayer flags and meditated above the upper stupa, just below the cave where the Seventh Dalai Lama practiced.

After a picnic lunch below the spot where Lama Drom often taught and where many of the early Dalai Lamas came to teach, I did a hike to the top of the nearby peak overlooking the temple, and then we returned to town. Lama Samdup Tsering, who had assisted us throughout the day, joined us on the bus ride back to the city. In the evening, we went for another walk around the Barkhor and meditated on the steps in front of it while the Tibetans did prostrations.

In the morning, we made pilgrimage to the Potala Palace, which had been built by the Fifth Dalai Lama on the old castle erected by Songtsen Gampo in the mid-seventh century. Although the government is a bit strict with activities in the Potala, we were allowed to sit for meditation in the main assembly hall, thanks to the kindness of the soldier on duty. After lunch in the Donyou Restaurant, we visited the Ani Tsankhung Nunnery. Again, we were allowed to sit in meditation while the nuns performed their chanting.

The next morning was inside the Jokhang, the first temple in Tibet. It was built in 639 CE by Songtsen Gampo to house the monks and Buddha statues brought by his Nepali wife.

The morning after, we took a one-and-a-half-hour drive to Ganden Monastery, where Tsongkhapa achieved enlightenment. We walked the *khorra*, which is a "revolution/circumambulation," around the hilltop and meditated in Tsongkhapa's meditation cave. Later we visited the monastery and meditated in the Sertung Lhakhang (Zhwa'i Lhakhang in Chinese), or Chapel of the Golden Reliquary, where the relics of Tsongkhapa's holy body are kept. On the way back to the city, we stopped for a picnic lunch near the Tsangpo River. We had a free afternoon. We used it to make a visit to the Ramoche Temple. This temple had been built in 641 CE by Songtsen Gampo to house the monks and Buddha statues brought to Tibet by his Chinese wife. We had a special audience with Ngak'chang Rinpoche, one of the most respected lamas in Tibet. At eighty-two years old, he hails from Tashi Lhunpo Monastery but lives and teaches in Lhasa. He is the only lama allowed to give public teachings in Central Tibet.

The day after was the flight from Lhasa to Beijing via Chengdu, followed by our return home the next day.

Tibet is presently a country that has been annexed into China. Its capital is Lhasa, which was also the seat of the Dalai Lama prior to his exile in Dharamshala, India. The Tibetan form of Buddhism has been spreading into Nepal, Bhutan, India, and even the West.

It is also true that as a religion gets established in a part of the world different from where it originated, it comes into contact with other philosophies, belief systems, religions, and environments; thus, some blending of ideas occurs. In China, the Yogacara division of Mahayana Buddhism came into contact with Taoism. This resulted in Chan Buddhism, which, when it transferred to Japan, became known as Zen. Even in a particular place of origin, a religion is born in the context of the local environment, ecology, religions, philosophies, political situations, and science of that region.

In the case of Tibetan Buddhism, the teaching of the Buddha came to Tibet during the time of the Dharma kings who were Songtsen Gampo, Trisong Detsen, and Ralpacan.[1] The first is the Yogacara school, established by Vasubandhu, involving the yogic practices to attain states of meditation.[2] The second is the Madhyamika school, promulgated by Nagarjuna, who was a Buddhist monk advocating a metaphysics based upon the Buddha's doctrine of the Middle Way, avoiding the extremes of asceticism and worldly overindulgence.[3]

In addition, the native religion of Bön contributed to the larger tapestry of the Tibetan forms of Buddhism, which developed into four schools.

Songtsen Gampo was the thirty-third Tibetan king and founder of the Tibetan Empire, who united what had previously been several Tibetan kingdoms.[4] He is credited with the introduction of Buddhism to Tibet, influenced by his Nepali consort Bhrikuti. During his reign, the translation of Buddhist texts from Sanskrit into Tibetan began. During the reign of Trisong Detsen in the eighth century, the Nyingma school was formally established. It is the oldest school of Buddhism in Tibet, founded by Vajrayana teacher Guru Padmasambhava, based upon translations of Buddhist scriptures from Sanskrit into Old Tibetan, which was the first dissemination of Buddhism into Tibet under Trisong Detsen.[5]

The Kadampa and Kargyütpa schools developed under the second dissemination. The Gelugpa school was established in the twelfth century, and it is that school that the Dalai Lama belongs to.[6]

These forms of Buddhism have also spread into the West. Of course, there were some people who traveled into Tibet in the nineteenth century and who allowed some understanding of Buddhism to reach the West. It has been since China annexed Tibet in 1950 that more of Tibetan Buddhism spread to other continents.

Meanwhile, there are other forms of Buddhism from Southeast Asia that have spread into Western nations. Even portions of the Tripitaka, the sacred texts of Buddhism, such as the Dhammapada, have made it into bookstores in Europe, North America, and other parts of the world. Another reasonably famous work is the *Bardo Thödol, The Tibetan Book of the Dead*, which is attributed to Padmasambhava.

It is important to interject here that the Christians have their Holy Bible, the Jews have their Torah, and the Islamic people their Koran. I have had the opportunity to read from cover to cover all of those works. This was undertaken as a scholarly and intellectual project that would allow me to understand the essence of those religions. I definitely find much inside those texts to be very inspirational and maybe even comforting; however, I do *not* consider any of those works to have been just dropped from the sky. There has always been a human—or many human—intermediaries involved.

I can*not* accept everything in the Bible as divinely inspired. As someone mentioned to me in one of our intellectual discussions, "The scriptures are *not* God! They are to be regarded as signposts to God!"

Just as there is a Bible, a Torah, and a Koran, the Zoroastrians have their Zend-Avesta, the Buddhists have the Tripitaka, the Taoists have the Tao Te Ching, the Confucians have the Confucian Analects, and the Hindus have the Hindu Vedas and Upanishads. I have been fortunate to have taken the time to study some of those writings. Likewise, they do contain literature, which is highly inspirational. There is much to be learned from those texts.

On that trip to Tibet, I had a chance to visit many Tibetan Buddhist monasteries. Having heard and read about the difficulties, trials, and tribulations of the Tibetan people, it is clear that the people inside Tibet are being oppressed by the Chinese government. On this trip, I had the opportunity to see this firsthand. Here I see two victims! Not only is it the Tibetan people who are victims. It is the Chinese people who are also victims of a communist authoritarian regime. Perhaps the present government is not quite as malignant as the regime of Mao Tse-tung during the Cultural Revolution; however, oppression still occurs. This has *not* ceased in the digital age, in which there are Microsoft, Google, and Apple. Because of the digital age, there can be greater transparency of information; however, the Chinese government has a nationwide firewall. This means, clearly, that this government censors much information.

When I was in Beijing, China, it was very clear to me how authoritarian the regime is. The communist symbols are everywhere. What changed is that, under a very highly regulated process, China has adopted many aspects of a capitalist free-enterprise system as it exists in the West. It is just that it is all controlled by the government. This is what allows any Chinese business to interface with and interact with any other business in the United States, Germany, Great Britain, France, or any other country.

Ultimately, the Chinese government wants to always maintain control of the operations of the government itself, businesses, corporations, nongovernmental organizations, and its people. Naturally, this is also a system that has contributed to environmental degradation.

Here, I would like to mention that, while I was on a trip circumnavigating the planet Earth, one leg of the trip was a flight from Bangkok, Thailand, to Frankfurt, Germany. It was during the morning as the airplane was flying over the Ural Mountains when I looked out the window, as it was dawn. I was curious since this was territory that had been part of the former Soviet Union. Although I have not been to any of the fifteen former Soviet republics, I was able to still appreciate some of the sights, looking over the landscape. It was good to see some of the forested areas, yet there were areas I saw that looked like a moonscape. During the seven decades of the Soviet communist rule, there was a great amount of environmental damage. Yes! The communist political philosophy and political ideology has *not* been kind to the environment. Just like the capitalism of the West, it has also exploited the resources of the planet.

Another trip that I have taken is to the southern part of the continent of Africa. On that trip, I traveled through Zambia, Zimbabwe, Botswana, Angola, Namibia, and South Africa. This was an extremely fascinating trip and an educational experience. These are countries that also possess their own histories.

Another quality that Donald Trump is renowned for is his thoughtless comments about other countries. Under the cloak of "Make America Great Again!" he made statements such as calling various countries around the world "shit-hole" countries. As a person who is a head of state, should he not present more respect toward other countries? I was glad when some of the leaders of some of those countries, including the president of Botswana, protested the use of such language. Having traveled through some of those countries, I have seen some astonishing beauty. In fact, some of those countries have some of the natural wonders of the planet. The Okavango Delta is one of those natural wonders, and it is in Botswana. The Victoria Falls are located on the Zambezi River, which is the international boundary between Zambia and Zimbabwe. Doesn't Donald Trump know about the Okavango Delta and the Victoria Falls? Does he *not* know that they are two of the natural wonders? I wonder!

Also important, I have started to study the history of some of the African nations, which goes back a long time. It was during the nineteenth century, when there was the scramble for Africa, that the European powers of that period of history partitioned the entire continent. It was an attempt to exploit the continent of its resources, as the European powers were competing among themselves over who would have a larger slice of the pie. Sometime after World War II, many of those African countries became independent, which would prove to have its own sets of challenges. Many of those countries do have a troubled history. Sometimes, despots would rule, and, under those despots, the resources of those countries would continue to be exploited, just like they were during colonial times. The people thus suffered under European power. Then they suffered under a despot or dictator. Think back to Idi Amin of Uganda! The despots would also mismanage the financial resources of the countries; hence, some countries would suffer from hyperinflation. I present this because I wonder if Donald Trump understands any of this history when he ascribes such derogatory labels to those countries.

To speak plainly, the fact that the African countries possess some outstanding beauty including natural wonders, which I have seen firsthand, does *not* make them shit-hole countries! It is unjust for Donald Trump to *not* understand the history and culture of any country and to use this type of language.

Instead of taking this type of hotheaded approach, doesn't it make more sense to make attempts at establishing better relations with other countries? Certainly! It is true that the United States, many European countries, and many Asian countries *do* have enemies and adversaries. Because of this, it is only prudent to maintain good relations with countries that the United Sates has good working relations with. Meanwhile it is important to establish good relations with other countries with which the connections are not that deep.

The relationship between Cuba and the United States from the time Fidel Castro came to power was either nonexistent or hostile; however, during Barack Obama's administration, the relationship started to thaw out. It was a positive sign that situations would improve and people would have the opportunity to travel between the two countries. If the United States has a cordial relationship with Vietnam, which is a communist country, then I don't see why it would be a problem to have more cordial relations between Cuba and the United States. It does *not* mean that I favor communism, since it is a political ideology that I disagree with. It only means having more cordial relations. In a world with organizations that are horrific, such as the Islamic State, it only makes sense to have as many friends as possible.

Unfortunately, during his presidency, Donald Trump wanted to backpedal on any progress made thus far with Cuba. This was unfortunate. Meanwhile, Donald Trump seemed to get cozy with other dictators, including Vladimir Putin. At the same time, he alienated many European allies. If anything, that gave Vladimir Putin exactly what he wanted, distrust and suspicion between the Western allies.

Here, I would like to add that, because the war in Iraq led to a greater destabilization of the Middle East, there have been massive migrations of people from the Middle East and northern Africa into Europe. Unfortunately, it has placed a great strain on the economic and social resources of many European countries. This, unfortunately, will not be resolved quickly.

In the United States, the immigration policies and laws are very conflicted. Donald Trump seemed to think that the "magic bullet" of building a wall was going to end the problem. The causes of the present problem goes back sevaral decades. As one of the causes, we have a situation where the conditions in some countries, such as Honduras, El Salvador, and Guatemala, are so depressed that people want to flee. This too is the result of exploitation, especially under dictators such as Ríos Montt of Guatemala. José Efraín Ríos Montt was a Guatemalan military officer and politician who served as the de facto president of Guatemala in 1982 to 1983. During his brief tenure as president, Guatemala experienced one of the bloodiest periods in the long-running civil war.[7] War crimes and genocide were conducted by the Guatemalan army under his leadership.

They exploited the people. With some of the dictators gone, many criminal drug gangs and other criminal organizations have taken over in some areas. These organizations do compete with each other, and they recruit. Some of the reasons why people have turned to crime are based on poverty. The drug trade is lucrative! Of course, In the United States, there are many people addicted to all types of drugs, such as opioids, heroin, amphetamines, and many others. This means there is a market in the United States. If there were no market in the United States, perhaps the drug cartels in Mexico and the drug gangs in Honduras, El Salvador, and Guatemala would vanish. Maybe not! This can't be known for certain.

Unfortunately, the reality is that Donald Trump's plan to build a wall did *not* make the problem go away. Build a wall, and there will always be ways to get over the wall, dig a tunnel under the wall, or find some other weakness in the wall.

I do not want to say that the problems are intractable; however, there will need to be a major multipronged approach. It will mean getting a handle on the problems with our educational system, which will require education on the effects of drug abuse and cigarette smoking. It is vital to have immigration reform. There will need to be much greater clarity with our asylum laws so that people fleeing political persecution can enter the United States at certain entry points legally. There must be a crackdown on corruption within the political systems in Mexico, Guatemala, El Salvador, and Honduras. Of course, it will mean a better working relationship between the United States and Mexico.

I traveled through Mexico and Guatemala, and, despite the impoverished conditions, it was still a fact that these countries were culturally rich. They also had their own natural wonders. I appreciated the hikes in El Pinacate Biosphere Reserve, with its volcanic moonlike topography. It was an accomplishment to achieve the summit of Popocatépetl, which is the second highest peak above sea level at 5,426 meters (17,802 feet). The sites of Tenochtitlan, Teotihuacan, and Tula allowed me to see the colossal statues of the civilizations of southern Mexico, such as the Toltecs and Aztecs. On another trip, I had the opportunity to visit the various Spanish missions of the Pimeria Alta, which included Magdalena, Imuris, Caborca, Pitiquito, and Cananea.

Yes, there is criminal activity, which anyone traveling through those countries needs to be concerned about. This does not mean that one has to live in fear. It does mean, be vigilant! Be aware! Travel as part of a group. Avoid those areas that are problematic. At the same time, you will find many good people in those countries who will be helpful. Last, do not believe Donald Trump's statements that they are all a bunch of criminals, rapists, etcetera. Some people may be that; however, those types of people are in the minority. One must never overgeneralize!

Chapter 4

ENVIRONMENTAL CROSSROADS

"Earth provides enough to satisfy every man's need,
but not every man's greed."
—Mohandas K. Gandhi, 1869–1945

Since I live in Tucson, Arizona, which is part of the Desert Southwest, I have come to appreciate the natural wonders of the planet Earth. Many times, I have backpacked in the Grand Canyon in Arizona. I have come to appreciate that there were some pioneer thinkers, such as Ralph Waldo Emerson, Henry David Thoreau, John Muir, and Theodore Roosevelt, who had great insight into protecting those lands that embody the essence of the natural world. How important it is to protect the larger ecology of the planet!

Inside the Grand Canyon, I was able to see the ages of the many rock layers. The oldest rocks, such as the Zoroaster Gneiss and Vishnu Schist, are somewhere from 1.5 to 1.7 billion—I repeat, *billion*—years old. The overlying rock structures are on the order of hundreds of millions of years old. It is so interesting to see those different sedimentary layers, such as the sandstone, limestone, and shale. With the erosion of the Grand Canyon occurring over the past five million years, the structures of the rock formations make for some very inspiring and aesthetic presentations. The rock formations have character! They have personality! Similar to the trek in the Himalayas, my experience of backpacking in the Grand Canyon was a test of physical endurance. Meanwhile, I also regard it as a spiritual endeavor. Now, when I undertake those adventures, I am appreciative of the fact that I have the good health, stamina, and ambition to allow me to proceed.

As I have traveled the world, I have seen many different climate zones, and they include the wettest places on Earth. They also include the most tropical places and the regions close to the arctic. They include being close to the centers of many continents, as well as tropical islands.

One of the fascinating and eye-opening trips was in the South Pacific to the island of Rapa Nui, which is also known as Easter Island (Isla de Pascua). The moai (carved human figures) were impressive. As I looked closely at the ecosystem, though, I saw many nonnative species present. Because it is just slightly south of the Tropic of Capricorn, one would envision an island that is lush with tropical or subtropical vegetation, including palm trees. Instead, I saw a barrenness to the island. About a year prior to that trip, I read Jared Diamond's book *Collapse: How Societies Choose to Fail or Succeed.*[1] A chapter in his book describes how the natives, through their internecine wars and exploitation of the natural resources, have devastated the island. I questioned our guide about that, and he mentioned to us that 96 percent of the plant species have been introduced to the island from elsewhere. Personally, I question the scenario of having the collapse being attributed to internecine warfare. Instead, I believe that the collapse happened *after* the arrival of the Europeans. Just as there was a scramble for Africa, there was a scramble for the South Pacific. A documentary, *Easter Island—Where Giants Walked*,[2] presents more convincing evidence, which is contrary to what Jared Diamond presents. Having read several of Jared Diamond's books, I know that he presents a lot of well-researched and correct information regarding many subjects. Unfortunately, in this particular case regarding the island of Rapa Nui, I can*not* agree with him.

It definitely came to my attention that the lakes, Rano Raraku and Rano Kau, are just a shadow of what they used to be. The man-made structures, such as Ahu Vinapu and Ahu Tongariki, are impressive; however, this is an ecosystem that has been damaged. Not only has it been damaged, it has collapsed!

My impression of Rapa Nui was that there were aspects to the island that intrigued me, yet, at the same time, I felt a sadness in that the damage that the human species can do is enormous. This left me thinking about what the human species is doing to the planet on a much larger scale.

On this trip, I continued on to Santiago and other parts of Chile. (Rapa Nui is a part of Chile.) Seeing the museums and plazas around Santiago, I was able to obtain a deeper understanding of the history of Chile, including episodes such as the War of the Pacific (1879–1883) and the overthrow of Salvador Allende by Augusto Pinochet. The good thing that I perceived is that now a democratic system has been in effect for quite a while. I saw people of various political parties, expressing various political views, present at the plazas. Also, various religious groups expressed their views. Even if I do not necessarily agree with a particular political view or religious view, it should still be expressed.

I continued south to do the ascent of Volcán Villarrica, near the town of Pucón. I had firsthand experience witnessing a volcanic action in progress. The ecosystem, high in the volcanic mountains, is a fragile one, and I saw how the plants survive until the snow line is reached. From this point upward, climbing is required, using an ice ax and crampons over glaciers to reach the summit. I could smell the fumes of the sulfur-containing compounds as I looked into the volcanic crater at the summit. Thin vaporous clouds were rising above the crater, and they contained sulfurous and sulfuric acid, which could cause a stinging and slight burning sensation in one's eyes.

I was reminded on this trip about another trip that I had done previously when I climbed to the summit of Mount Kilimanjaro, which is the highest point above sea level in Africa. It also reminded me of the tundra in the Yukon Territory in Canada. The commonality was the fragility of the ecosystems, despite the fact that they are in geographically different parts of the world. At the same time, experiencing the fumes from the volcano's venting its fumes, I could see how powerful nature is. These volcanoes were built up over long periods of time, changing the landscapes. Different processes may be operating, as Mount Kilimanjaro resulted from the rift widening in Africa, and Volcán Villarrica resulted from the Nazca plate being subducted under the continent of South America, forming the Andes, including its many volcanoes.

I continued south to the Parque Nacional Alerce Andino. This was an important highlight, as it allowed me to hike into another one of the temperate rainforests of the world. The alerce tree (*Fitzroya cupressoides*),[3] in the plant family *Cupressaceae*, is related to the sequoia and redwood trees of California. The alerce trees are as far south of the equator as the sequoias and redwood are north of the equator. This fact is extremely interesting!

I ask myself how plants in the same family have evolved to be in similar regions of the planet, yet so distantly removed from each other geographically. Of course, there is convergent evolution, where plants or animals of entirely different families can acquire similar characteristics. This is why cacti (*Cactaceae*) and spurge euphorbs (*Euphoriaceae*) possess similar fleshy xerophytic plant tissue. Meanwhile, hiking through the forest in Chile allowed me to see and understand similarities with plants that I know about in the Sonoran and Chihuahuan Deserts.

Crossing the international boundary into Argentina, I could see the scenery of Patagonia. Photos and videos do not do justice to actually being there. This is true of so many places that I have been to. This is why I take the opportunity to get to those places. Parque Nacional de Cerro Tronador and Parque Nacional Nahuel Huapi were outstandingly beautiful. Being on opposite sides of the Andes, I could see how different those two national parks are from Parque Nacional Alerce Andino. In addition, stopping in to visit the towns of Osorno and Frutillar in Chile and San Carlos de Bariloche in Argentina, I could see how those various communities blend into the surrounding landscape.

As in the United States where there were visionary people who had the idea of establishing national parks, it was pleasing to see that Chile and Argentina also had their own visionaries who wanted to set aside lands to be protected, instead of having them plowed away and their natural resources exploited. This was in many ways a contrast to what I was seeing elsewhere in the world. It was very different from Rapa Nui.

On a prior trip to South America, I was able to actually spend some time in the Amazon of Peru and Brazil. It was there where I renewed my interest in the flora—and to some degree, the fauna—of the planet. As all my trips are an education, this one proved to be an exceptional learning experience. There was so much to be learned about the cultures of those rainforests of Peru, as I was spending some time with the Yagua, Yanomami, and Bora tribes. They may be regarded as primitive; however, they understand things that we in the Western world do not understand. They are grounded to the Earth and Mother Nature. The tropical rainforest is a walk-in pharmacy, and the people inhabiting the rainforest have an understanding of the uses of its plants. They are highly educated with this profound understanding. As a visitor and an outsider to their world, I realized how little I knew. Even though I consider myself an intellectual and educated, it was an experience that showed me how much more I needed to learn.

Of course, as I crossed the international boundary into Brazil, I did see large areas of deforestation. This reminded me of a conversation that I had had on a trip to Australia several years earlier. I was in the Ikara-Flinders Ranges National Park, and I met a man who had traveled through Brazil. He told me about what he witnessed: fires burning down the forest! Now I saw some of the results of the handiwork of those people—and greedy corporations—behind the decimation of the forests. Yes, it is real!

Since my trip to South America, I have had time to digest what I have experienced. This has led me to keep asking: What is the direction we are headed into? Being back home now, I continue my intellectual pursuits, realizing that I will never come close to understanding what some indigenous people understand.

Then I ask myself: What type of a society are we living in? This is in addition to what direction we are headed into. We don't even have an interest in what is to be learned from the tropical rainforests, as they are being cleared away because of corporate greed. As of 2018, 8 percent of the original rainforests remain in Brazil. Of course, in other parts of the world, such as Africa, Southeast Asia, Indonesia, and elsewhere, the picture does not look so bright either. Many species are being lost! If a plant species containing a compound that could be of value becomes extinct, we have indeed truly lost something of value.

Here, I will refer back to my trip to Rapa Nui, where the landscape of the island is barren. On that island, there is a fungus that produces the antifungal rapamycin.[4] It was named after the island of Rapa Nui. This is a compound that has been found to have applications in cancer chemotherapy and immunosuppression. This compound is an example of many. Other compounds are vincristine and vinblastine, which are utilized in cancer chemotherapy. They originate from the Vinca or periwinkle plant (family *Apocynaceae*) in Madagascar.[5] This is an island where extensive deforestation is also occurring.

Furthermore, the indigenous people in the Amazon can teach us many other things, such as how to live life. To them, nature is *not* something to be exploited and pushed aside. They live in balance with their surrounding environment. They recognize that they do *not* have dominance over nature. Many shamans, whether they are from tribes in the Amazon, Native American tribes, African tribes, the Australian Aborigines, or many others, have come to recognize these truths.

What would happen should the tropical rain forests vanish? The consequences would be dismal. As there are tribes still retaining their original lifeways to this day, their cultures would vanish. Many Native American languages have been lost, and more are in jeopardy of dying out. It is good to see that some cultures have retained their identity, despite the misfortunes of history, and are asserting their rights to retain, study, learn, and teach their languages. Even on my trips to Hawaii, I spoke with some native Hawaiian people, and they were telling me how they now have to learn Hawaiian as their second language. Truly sad!

Definitely, I find it ludicrous that people of any culture are robbed of their languages and forced to learn another. Then their languages are regarded as their second languages. Yes, ludicrous indeed! The only good thing is that there are efforts to preserve the native languages that have not been lost. It reminds me of studying the history of the North American Indian tribes, and they were forced onto reservations. Often, the children were disciplined for speaking their native languages.

As mentioned above, I have been to Qatar, as I was en route on a trip to the southern part of Africa. It was in Africa that I saw some spectacular beauty that included two of the natural wonders of the Earth: Victoria Falls and the Okavango Delta.

Here I shall explain the details of another one of my interesting trips. The flights were such that it was one half hour from Tucson to Phoenix; two hours from Phoenix to Houston; fifteen hours on Qatar Airlines from Houston to Doha, Qatar; eight hours from Qatar to Johannesburg, South Africa; and two hours on British Airways from Johannesburg to Livingstone, Zambia. Arriving at the airport in Livingstone, I passed through Zambian customs quickly since I already had my visas in order. I spent a couple of nights at the Zambezi Waterfront Lodge, which is right on the Zambezi River and several kilometers upstream from Victoria Falls. The sun was shining with some cloudiness, and I was told that the rainy season was just about to start. The air was very warm, tropical, and slightly humid.

I made arrangements to prepare to go to Victoria Falls National Park inside Zimbabwe. The next morning after breakfast, I crossed the international border to visit Victoria Falls, which is one of the seven natural wonders on this Earth. It was wonderful! I saw the falls, the deep gorge that had been cut by the Zambezi River, some vervet monkeys, colorful birds, and some interesting species of plants, such as the baobab trees. I even saw some agave, which was imported into Zimbabwe and is found naturally in Arizona. There was also a statue of David Livingstone in the southern part of the park. It was after David Livingstone that they named the town of Livingstone in Zambia. Since I had my visas in order, the border crossings were quick and smooth.

The next day, I left the lodge early to be part of a lion walk. We encountered two female lions, which we had the opportunity to pet. This was part of a lion conservation program to reintroduce lions into the wild because of vast reduction in numbers throughout Africa and habitat destruction. I also learned about some interesting species of plants, such as maerua (*Maerua schinzii Pax,* family *Capparaceae*),[6] mubuyu, mbula, mubombo, flame tree (*Erythrina abyssinica),*[7] mutoto (*Rauvolfia caffra,* family *Apocynaceae*),[8] and ochna (*Ochna pulchra,* family *Ochnaceae*)[9]. After, I checked out of the Zambezi Waterfront Lodge and transferred to the Bushfront Lodge, I had the afternoon to visit the Livingstone Museum, which had lots of good information about the natural history of Zambia and an interesting section about the colonial historical period through independence and what had happened since independence. There was an interesting subsection about the life of David Livingstone.

The next morning, I met the other group members, and we visited the Zambian side of Victoria Falls, It provided a different perspective of the falls from which we were able to see colorful rainbows. In fact, very briefly, I observed a double rainbow. I saw some other interesting plants, such as the thorn tree and jacaranda trees. (Jacaranda is a genus of forty-nine species of flowering plants in the family *Bignoniaceae*, which is native to tropical and subtropical regions of South America [Argentina, Brazil, and Uruguay], Central America, Mexico, and the Caribbean. It has been introduced to Australia, New Zealand, India, Fiji, and parts of Africa.)[10] In fact the national park had interpretive signs that presented many of the ecological problems regarding introduced plant species that have become invasive, such as lantana.

We crossed the international border at the Kazungula border post from Zambia to Botswana, which took more than two hours because they had to ferry us—and our safari van—across the Zambezi River. We checked into the Thebe River Lodge, from where we went on a boat cruise on the Chobe River, which is a tributary of the Zambezi River, upstream into Chobe National

Park. The opportunities were excellent to see hippopotamuses, elephants, impalas, cape buffalo, warthogs, crocodiles, monitor lizards, egrets, kites, vultures, baobab trees, and much more. The next morning, we took a jeep drive inside Chobe National Park, where we saw much of what we had seen on the boat the day before; however, we had the added opportunity to see lions, hyenas, giraffes, sables, kudus, banded mongooses, guinea fowl, bee-eater birds, saddle-billed storks, and other birds. From Chobe National Park, we crossed the border into Namibia, staying the night at the Namushasha River Lodge, which is along the Kwando River, which subsequently flows into the Okavango Delta.

We departed the Namushasha River Lodge and drove a short distance in the East Caprivi District of Namibia to the town of Divundu. Then we went south into Botswana, where we went to the town of Sepupa. We then took a speedboat to a houseboat and spent two nights there. The next morning, we took the speedboat from the houseboat to Seronga, where several of us booked a flight over the Okavango Delta. We took canoes into the wetlands of the delta, where we saw elephants, hippopotamuses, plovers, egrets, kingfishers, fish eagles, pentagrid frogs, and other bird species. We also had a treat as far as plant species are concerned, such as sausage tree (*Kigelia africana,* family *Bignoniaceae*),[11] rain tree (*Lonchocarpus capassa,* family *Fabaceae*),[12] baobab (*Adansonia digitata,* family *Bombacoideae*),[13] and marula (*Sclerocarya birrea,* family *Anacardiaceae*)[14]. After lunch, those of us who booked the flight had the opportunity to fly over and see the Okavango Delta. Seeing the delta from the sky provided the added perspective of seeing the larger ecosystem and hydrology of that region, which is the northern part of the Kalahari Desert. Having this opportunity provided one of the highlights of the trip, which was to see the Okavango Delta, another one of the seven natural wonders of this world. From the plane, we could also see elephants, hippopotamuses, giraffes, and buffalo. This flight was followed by a sunset cruise.

We woke up to experience a wonderful sunrise. We returned via the speedboat to Sepupa. From there, we crossed back from Botswana into Namibia. We continued to Rundu, where we stood at a lodge right along the Cubango River, which is the Angolan name for the Okavango River, which flows into the delta. There, the river is the international boundary between Namibia and Angola. We took a sunset cruise on that river, anchoring the boat on the Angolan side of the river, and walked on the Angolan side, taking photographs of the sunset. There were also some cumulonimbus clouds in the distance with lightning. After the cruise during dinner, we saw a native African dance that included African drum music.

After breakfast, I photographed some plants, such as the leopard orchid (*Ansellia Africana*, family *Orchidaceae*),[15] bougainvillea (*Nyctaginaceae*),[16] frangipani (*Apocynaceae*),[17] and heliconia (*Heliconiaceae*)[18]. We left Rundu, stopping in Grootfontein and continuing to Etosha National Park. This was another place where a lot of wildlife could be observed, especially giraffes, springboks, kudus, oryx, zebras, elephants, jackals, and lions. The evening was concluded with a short hike to a water hole, where rhinoceroses and elephants could be seen at night drinking. Then I did a little stargazing at some of the summer constellations of the southern hemisphere. The planet Jupiter and the nearby star Achernar were shining brightly.

Before breakfast, we went on an early-morning drive to observe more wildlife, which was an opportune time to see much of the game in abundance, especially at the water holes. In the afternoon, there was some free time to visit the water hole and other places around the campgrounds, where I was able to photograph birds, squirrels, geckos, and plants. We went on an afternoon drive to several water holes and the Etosha Pan to see more wildlife. At one of the water holes, there was a family reunion of lions scaring away the giraffe and other game animals from the water. Afterward, we did a hike up one of the dolomite hills, where I could photograph a small forest of Moringa trees (*Moringa ovalifolia*, family *Moringaceae*),[19] which have a vague resemblance to the Bursera and elephant trees (*Bursera microphylla*, family *Burseraceae*)[20] in Arizona. The Moringa tree was an interesting, unusual, and strange-looking tree that provided the hill with a fairytale landscape appearance. We saw another colorful sunset from that forest. The evening provided another clear sky for astronomy.

After breakfast, we went on another drive to some water holes, where we saw more game animals and lions. We stayed the night at the Okaukuejo campground, where there was another water hole for observing elephants, rhinoceroses, and game animals taking their turns at drinking from the water hole. That morning, I also climbed up a tower where I could photograph some of the surrounding landscape. Some of the other plants of Etosha National Park that I learned about are the mopane (*Colophospermum mopane*, family *Fabaceae*),[21] rooibos (*Combretum apiculatum*, family *Combretaceae*),[22] *Rhus marlothii* (family *Anacardiaceae*),[23] and *Gymnosporia senegalensis* (family *Celastraceae*)[24]. We left Etosha National Park for Khorixas, where we spent the night.

We left Khorixas for the Petrified Forest Preserve. In addition to seeing lots of petrified wood, we saw lots of Welwitschia plants and Commiphora trees (*Commiphora glandulosa*, family *Burseraceae*).[25] (Note: The Welwitschia is a monotypic genus of gymnosperm plant, composed solely of *Welwitschia mirabilis*.[26] It is the only genus of the family *Welwitschiaceae*, in the order Welwitschiales, in the division Gnetophyta.) The commiphora trees reminded me of the Moringa trees back in Etosha National Park. This was the part of Namibia where the topography, with its mountains and

Brandberg Massif—the high point of Namibia (2,573 meters)—became interesting. We continued through this interesting landscape to Twyfelfontein, where we saw the native rock engravings in the sandstone rocks. Much of the rock art represented various creatures found in the region. We continued to Uis, where we spent the night, and I had another opportunity to teach some astronomy.

As we departed Uis to Cape Cross on the Atlantic coast, we had another grand opportunity to view Brandberg as we headed west. We arrived at Cape Cross on the Skeleton Coast, where we saw the cape fur seals—thousands of them. We also stopped at one of the shipwrecks along the Skeleton Coast on the drive south to Swakopmund. Once we arrived in Swakopmund, I signed up for the dolphin cruise. Afterward, I visited the museum, which had lots of interesting historical displays and presentations pertaining to the German colonial times. The next morning, I went on that dolphin cruise, where we saw jellyfish, pelicans, flamingos, gulls, other shorebirds, seals, one elephant seal, and—of course—dolphins. Too bad the aquarium in Swakopmund was closed for renovation.

We left Swakopmund for Walvis Bay, where we viewed and photographed some of the bird life, such as the flamingos. We continued east into the Namib Desert, where we saw more interesting landscapes and sand dunes. We had a quick stop in Solitaire for refreshments, continuing to our next lodge where we were surrounded by scenic vistas. We woke up early for the drive to the sand dunes at Sossusvlei. It was interesting to see and photograph the dunes after the sunrise. We had an excellent guide who provided a lot of information about the sand dunes, the mammals (oryx, gerbils, and moles), insects (several beetle species), plants (kanna [*Mesembryanthemum tortuosum*, family *Aizoaceae*]),[27] oryx cucumber, and tsamo melon), and birds. The guide led us on a short hike to some of the dunes and flats, where the water collects during the rainy season and dries out, leaving the calcium deposits behind. It was also educational to hear about the formation and origin of the sand dunes, taking into account the geology, the ocean currents, and weather patterns. After the guided hike, I did a hike on my own up one of the sand dunes. After lunch, several of us went on a guided hike down Sesriem Canyon, which looks similar to Sycamore Canyon near Nogales, Arizona; however, the rocks in Sesriem Canyon consisted of conglomerate and sandstone. There was even a pool in one of the side canyons. Also, we saw several interesting plants, such as the quiver trees. That night, I woke up early, so that I could view the stars. This time, I saw the Magellanic Clouds, Achernar, Canopus, the Southern Cross, the Milky Way, and other southern hemisphere stars and constellations.

We left the Namib-Naukluft National Park to visit the cheetah preserve, where we saw caracals, a leopard, and several cheetahs. We also had the opportunity to play with the cheetahs. We continued on the long drive to Fish River Canyon. Just like the Grand Canyon in Arizona and Las Barrancas del Cobre in Mexico, this is also one of the largest canyon systems in the world. The geological history of this canyon is interesting since its oldest rocks are two billion years old. We saw another great sunset at the rim of that canyon.

Leaving the Fish River Canyon, we crossed the international border from Namibia into South Africa on the Orange River. We stayed in Okiep, which is in the wine country, for the night. We continued south to Cape Town, seeing some more interesting landscapes in the South African wine country and the Cederberg Mountains. We arrived in Cape Town in the late afternoon, where we did a walk to the waterfront and saw another nice sunset.

The next day, I went on a tour to Cape Point and the Cape of Good Hope. The tour guide was very knowledgeable about many aspects of South Africa. We stopped at a couple of good vista points, such as Clifton Bay and Camps Bay, the Twelve Apostles, and some other points, where we could see seals, penguins, a hyrax, and even a whale from the distance. We stopped at Cape Point for lunch and had an excellent opportunity to view the ocean from the lighthouse. From there, we went to the Cape of Good Hope, where we also saw several ostriches. On the return to Cape Town, we briefly stopped at the Kirstenbosch National Botanical Gardens.

The next day I took the "Blue" city tour bus to various locations in downtown Cape Town and then spent most of the day at the Kirstenbosch National Botanical Gardens, in detail. The highlight of that was the many colorful protea and Strelitzia plants. There were also many other plants that had adapted to both wet and dry conditions at the gardens.

During this trip to the southern part of the African continent, I saw many natural wonders, which included the spectacular wildlife. Like in South America, it is good that many African countries have come to the realization that it is important to set up their own national park systems.

The idea of a national park was an excellent idea that originated in the United States. With that innovation that allowed wilderness areas to be protected, many other countries around the world on many continents have adopted the concept of a national park. No doubt, the administration facilities and the means of overseeing the parks vary from country to country. Fundamentally, the idea is to protect wilderness and wildlife, along with their respective flora and fauna.

During the Obama administration, many federal lands were provided with an extra level of protection by being designated wilderness areas. This was an extremely positive accomplishment.

I have taken many road trips through all of the western United States. All of them possess their own intrinsic beauty. I did a backpacking trip in Yellowstone National Park, which is the first national park to have been established in the United States (the act of Congress was signed into law on March 1, 1872). It has such fascinating geology and topography; there are geysers, hot springs, and water holes to be found everywhere. In fact, many of those sites contain interesting life forms in the domain Archaea. They can withstand extremes of heat, pH, and chemical composition, which would kill most other life. We should be thankful to those people who made the right decision to set aside this land as a national park.

On the return home, I passed through regions in southern Utah and northern Arizona. This is red-rock country with geologic layers that are contiguous with the layers in the Grand Canyon in Arizona. It is some of this land that was designated as national monuments under the Obama administration. One example is the Bears Ears National Monument. Since I had traveled through these lands on many road trips, I was able to see some of them prior to the time they were designated with national monument status.

With the Trump administration, these national monuments were under threat. Donald Trump wanted to effect executive orders that shrank the land areas designated with national monument status or even eliminate some of them. The difference between a national monument and a national park is that the president of the United States can designate certain lands as a national monument by invoking the Antiquities Act or through some other mechanism. A national-park designation requires an act of Congress. Here is a brief overview of the Antiquities Act, as explained on the Department of the Interior's public documents:

> The Antiquities Act was the first US law to provide general legal protection of cultural and natural resources of historic or scientific interest on federal lands. After a generation-long effort, President Theodore Roosevelt signed

the Antiquities Act on June 8, 1906. The Antiquities Act set an important precedent by asserting a broad public interest in the preservation of these resources on federal lands. Designations under the Act apply only to federal lands; they place no restrictions on private property and have not affected valid existing rights.

After signing it into law, President Roosevelt used the Antiquities Act eighteen times to establish national monuments. Those first monuments included what are now known as Grand Canyon National Park, Petrified Forest National Park, Chaco Culture National Historical Park, Lassen Volcanic National Park, Tumacacori National Historical Park, and Olympic National Park.

Since President Roosevelt, sixteen US presidents have used the Act over 150 times to establish or expand national monuments. Congress may also pass legislation designating national monuments. Currently, the National Park Service manages eighty-three national monuments. The Bureau of Land Management administers twenty-five national monuments. And the US Fish and Wildlife Service administers six national monuments.

The Antiquities Act has a proven track record of protecting significant Federal lands and the unique cultural and natural resources they possess. These monuments have become universally revered symbols of America's beauty and legacy. Though some national monuments have been established amidst controversy, who among us today would dam the Grand Canyon, turn Muir Woods over to development, or deny the historic significance of Harriet Tubman's struggle against slavery? These sites are cherished landscapes that help to define the American spirit. They speak eloquently to the wisdom of retaining the Antiquities Act in its current form.[28]

Once again, the Trump agenda to eliminate some national monuments was in accordance with certain campaign promises to work with the oil, gas, coal, and mining industries. It seems so simple for someone with limited intellect to remove lands from national monument or wilderness status to allow for exploitation of our natural resources, which may or may not exist in those lands. This is an example of fulfilling a campaign promise to support corporate greed.

We are indeed at a crossroads, and, as I continue to understand the natural world better and how the human species is doing damage to the ecosystems of the planet, I am aware that much more conservation work needs to be done. One of the things that I learned from several of my trips is how humans have done environmental damage in the past.

On one of those trips, I was in the Yucatan in Mexico, Belize, and Guatemala. The theme of this trip was to learn more about the Mayan civilization. This allowed me to visit the ruins of Tulum, Caracol, La Blanca, Xunantunich, Yaxhá, and Tikal.

Starting with a flight from Tucson to Houston, I continued on another flight from Houston to Cancun, Mexico, arriving in the late afternoon. From there, I took the bus to Playa del Carmen, where I spent several days. With several of the people in our group, I ate a fish dinner at a restaurant along the beach. There was a fresh tropical breeze. I spent the next day walking the streets of Playa del Carmen, taking in the sights and hiking along the beach. The day after, I visited the Mayan ruins of Tulum, which was one of the sites along the coast, was not abandoned, and was still active at the time of the arrival of the Spanish. There were also lots of iguanas at that Mayan site.

We took the bus south from Playa del Carmen to Chetumal, where we crossed the international border from Mexico into Belize. From the border, we took another bus to Belize City, which is right on the Caribbean coast. From there, we took a boat ride to the island of Caye Caulker, which is past the barrier reef. It is the second largest coral reef system in the world after the Great Barrier Reef in Australia. I went snorkeling at three different locations nearby for an entire day as part of a group. We saw sea turtles, stingrays, nurse sharks, barracudas, moray eels, many other species of colorful fish, and many other creatures of the reef. The guide even caught and held one of the nurse sharks, allowing us to touch the creature. We also saw a beautiful bright red sunset. That evening, I had barracuda steaks for dinner. Later that night, I spent some time looking at the stars. Being farther south in latitude, I could easily see Canopus much higher in the sky than in Tucson, where it would be very low above the horizon when one faces the southern direction. I also saw Achernar. I had the opportunity to teach some of the people in our group and others some astronomy and show them the constellations, the stars, and the location of the Andromeda galaxy. The next day, I visited other parts of the island, such as a nature preserve, and I spent some time photographing the plants.

We left Caye Caulker by boat for Belize City. There we took the bus through the capital city of Belmopan and on to San Ignacio. Several of us made arrangements to visit the Mayan ruins of Caracol. The next day, we headed south to the Chiquibul National Park, where Caracol was located. The guide explained many details of the history of Caracol, including its battles with Tikal and how the Maya had deforested the land during classic times (300–900 CE). The jungle had grown back since. What was interesting about the site was the combination of the Mayan ruins and the tropical vegetation. Some of the interesting plants were the ceiba trees, the gumbo-limbo, taro, and the bromeliad epiphytes. Returning to

San Ignacio, we stopped to do a short hike in the Maya Mountains to some waterfalls.

We left San Ignacio, continuing west to the international border with Guatemala. Right near the border, we could see the Mayan ruins Xunantunich. After taking care of the border formalities of leaving Belize and entering Guatemala, we continued west, where we visited the ruins of La Blanca and Yaxhá. It was at those two sites where we learned about how the Mayans heated the limestone to make the mortar to cement the stones for their building projects. This, in turn, exploited the resources of the forest, resulting in deforestation. We then continued to Flores, where we spent the night.

The next day after breakfast, we embarked on a jungle trek for four days, where we hiked through the Protected Biotope El Zotz and Tikal National Park. The guides explained to us many interesting things about the many plants in the tropical rainforest. Most have many different types of medicinal properties. These include antimalarials, snake-venom antidotes, antitoxins against other poisonous plants, and many others of an ethnobotanical nature. There were several smaller Mayan ruins that we visited, and around sunset of the first night, we visited la Cueva de los Murciélagos, which is "the cave of the bats." Just around sunset at those cliffs and caves, there were two species of bats that leave to go feeding during the night. As those bats were flying away, they were very close to us, and we could feel their wings touch us. They felt like velvet. Later after dinner, I took time to observe the stars since the skies were very clear. During the night, we often heard the howler monkeys. During the day, we often saw spider monkeys and howler monkeys. We also saw various species of birds, such as the oropendolas and their hanging nests.

We arrived at the Mayan ruins of Tikal through the jungle. It was there where we saw some coatimundi and wild turkey. I spent the rest of the day exploring the large complex of temples, taking extra time at the larger and steeper temples. This was the highlight of all the Mayan ruins that we saw. We stayed at a campground at Tikal that had an even better view of the sunset and the night sky, because we were in an open space and had a larger section of the sky visible, compared to being in the tropical forest. The next morning, I explored the crocodile pond and visited the two small museums. I also saw some toucans.

After our return to Flores, I walked around the town, and it was a time when they were having festivals. Flores is on an island that is connected via a bridge to the town of Santa Elena. I visited the main church at the highest point on the island, the market, and a couple of bookstores. It was interesting to see how the prices of books dropped radically from the prices of those same books at the gift shops at Tikal. We also watched a slide presentation from an authority on Mayan architecture.

We continued south to the town of Rio Dulce, which is located right where Lago de Izabal empties into the Rio Dulce, and then took a boat to visit a Spanish fort that was used to protect the territory against British pirates. Then we continued downstream to the town of Livingston, which is on the Caribbean. I visited a cave that had some stalactites and stalagmites. There were lots of birds to be seen, such as cormorants, pelicans, gulls, frigate birds, and other species. We returned to the town of Rio Dulce, where we stopped at a preserve that had sea turtles.

We continued west passing through Guatemala City. This is a city that is renowned for its high criminal activities. About five murders a day occur there. We were just passing through on our way to Antigua de Guatemala, an old Spanish colonial town that is significant for its old Spanish architecture.

An important highlight was the trip to Volcán Pacaya. I left Antigua very early the next day to join a group going on a hike up the volcano. The drive to the trailhead was about one and a half hours. We hiked for about three kilometers to the lava flows. Although we were not at the summit where the red-hot lava was flowing, it was very high. Also, the summit was smoking. We could feel the heat from the red-hot lava, and one of the guides stuck a stick into the hot lava, and it ignited instantly into flames. The solidified lava took on many interesting forms and shapes.

I also visited the markets in Chichicastenango and Antigua before returning home.

Although it was true that many of the primitive tribes had a healthy respect for the natural world that supported them, such was not universally true. The Mayan civilization, which was very advanced for their time, even had sophisticated mathematics, geometry, architecture, and art. The people were very literate. Many of its city-states possessed an elite group that was supported by strong religious institutions and a military-industrial complex. There was much rivalry between the various city-states, with shifting alliances. As a result of constant warfare, the resources of the region were exploited. Because of a combination of the quest for empire and the exploitation of resources, the political system became overextended. The final result was collapse.

During the ninth to twelfth centuries, the deforestation of those regions of southern Mexico and Central America was extensive. After the collapse of the Mayan civilization, the rainforest did reclaim the abandoned lands. This is why today one finds some temple structures that appear to be small hills and are covered with vegetation. Underneath the vegetation are the ruins of temples and city structures. What one sees today as one is traveling through sites such as Tikal and Caracol are structures that have been uncovered by archaeologists. In many ways, the vegetation cover has protected the underlying structures from further damage. The tourist sees structures that are well manicured and maintained to support the tourist business. Archaeological research is continually being conducted, as there is more to be learned, including the Mayan civilization. Sometimes, I came across sections of a site that were partitioned off because of archaeological digs and research that were underway. Such archaeological and scientific research has helped to elucidate the history of those civilizations, including gaining a better understanding of the ecological damage that has been done.

More recently, I was on another trip to South America during which I was in Ecuador. There, I spent time in Quito before heading to the Galapagos Islands.

I arrived in Quito, Ecuador, and stayed at the Mercure Alameda Hotel in downtown Quito. The next day, one of the guides picked three of us up for a tour of Quito. The tour started with a visit to an open market where there were all types of fruits and vegetables. Many represent different cultivars of potatoes, maize (corn), and bananas. The market also had a section that contained a variety of herbs, spices, and medicinal plants. There was also a *curandera* present, who performed a cleansing of one of the people in our group using some incense, herbs, and oils. This represents a practice among indigenous people who engage in holistic healing. From there, we went to Ciudad Mitad del Mundo, where one could literally stand on both sides of the equator and be in both hemispheres at the same time. We returned to the downtown area, where we visited the Plaza Mayor, some churches, and some cathedrals that had Spanish Baroque and Andalusian mixtures of architectural styles. The day ended with a visit to Museo Nacional del Ecuador, which had historical exhibits originating prior to Inca times, during Inca times, during the Spanish colonial period, and from Ecuador after its independence.

We departed Quito via Guayaquil to the Galapagos Islands.

We landed on Isla Baltra, where we boarded the *Tip Top IV* yacht. After lunch, we went on a hike on the northern tip of Baltra and North Seymour Island. There were many marine iguanas to be seen. Also, several lava lizards were present. Bird life was abundant everywhere. The predatory frigate birds, also known as the pirate ships of the air, were flying around everywhere. Many of those frigate birds were also nesting in the trees and bushes. The males displayed the bright red inflated balloon-like sac, which is displayed during courtship. There were quite a few blue-footed boobies, various species of finches, and lava gulls. We also saw some land iguanas. There were quite a few sea lions present, with one nursing its pup. Importantly, there was a forest of incense trees (*Bursera graveolens*, family *Burseraceae*),[29] and it is also known as palo santo.

The next day, we had an early start with a hike on Isla Genovesa, where we had the opportunity to see some interesting geologic formations and tide pools. We saw some tiny crabs, which live in tiny holes in the ground, and they are often food for the herons, which we saw a lot of also. We saw a lot of frigate birds, whether flying or nesting. There were many red-footed boobies, cactus finches, ground finches, yellow warblers, and mockingbirds. There were also prickly pear cacti growing from various crevices in the lava rock. There was also a red-colored sesuvium (*Sesuvium edmonstonei*, family *Aizoaceae*),[30] known as carpet weed, and it forms dense carpets over sandy or rocky terrain. Sea lions were seen everywhere. Then, we went snorkeling for about an hour, where we saw an assortment of fish of all sizes, colors, and species, as well as sea urchins. Among some of the fish were groupers, angelfish, hawkfish, blenny, parrotfish, and many other species. In the afternoon, we did another hike on another part of the island, which involved a short steep section. We were able to see many different birds, including several species we hadn't seen before, such as green-footed boobies and tropic birds.

We saw some *chamaesyce* (*Euphorbia amplexicaulis*, family *Euphorbiaceae*)[31] plants, which are euphorbes, and more marine iguanas, which appeared to be piled on top of one another.

We arrived at Isla Santiago, where we started with a hike after breakfast to the Minas de Sal area. The path led us to an area with igneous rock formed from many lava flows. There were many crabs, pelicans, marine iguanas, sea lions, frigate birds, warblers, finches, a hawk, and other species of birds present. There were also several interesting plants. An example is the Galapagos croton (*Croton scouleri*, family *Euphorbiaceae*),[32] which is a small tree or shrub with yellow-white flowers. Another interesting plant is muyuyo, or yellow cordia (*Cordia lutea*, family *Boraginaceae*),[33] which is related to Texas olive. It is a small tree that produces yellow flowers and fruits. They are the main sources of nectar for the Galapagos sulfur butterfly and the Galapagos carpenter bee. There were also lava tubes in the volcanic structure, and, where the rock had collapsed, a bridge formed. From a distance, we were able to see manta rays surfacing. This was followed by a boat ride to a location where sea turtles were present. We went to Playa Espumilla, where we saw some ghost crabs and learned about the mangroves. There are two species: button mangrove (*Conocarpus erectus*, family *Combretaceae*)[34] and red mangrove (*Rhizophora mangle*, family *Rhizophoraceae*)[35]. I did some kayaking up the coast, where we saw some interesting geological features, which included some sea caves and lava formations. The day ended well with a sighting of manta rays that seemed curious about our presence.

When we arrived at Isla Isabela, we took a boat ride along some cliffs at Punta Vicente Roca, which had some more interesting geologic formations consisting of dikes, sea caves, and layers of different colors and inclination. We saw several sea turtles swimming in the waters, and there were lots of cormorants, along with many other species of birds, perched along the cliffs. We continued sailing south, where many frigate birds approached the boat and even perched on it. I managed to take some good photos of those birds. We also saw humpback whales, which I also managed to photograph. In the afternoon, we went to Punta Espinosa on Isla Fernandina, where we saw marine iguanas swimming, along with flightless cormorants and herons. We also had a nice view of La Cumbre volcano on Isla Fernandina.

Back on Isla Isabela, we did a landing at Tagus Cove, where the site had historical graffiti from the nineteenth and early twentieth centuries. From there, we hiked on a trail that brought us above Darwin Lake and a vista point, where more lava flows could be seen. Darwin Lake is a landlocked deep lake on Isla Isabela, which has an elevation a little higher than sea level and contains salt water. In fact the salinity of the water is about double that of ocean water.[36] In the afternoon, we went to Elizabeth Bay, where we sailed through the mangrove forest and other areas along the shore. We saw lots of Galapagos penguins, sea turtles, sea lions, pelicans, and even a Peruvian torpedo ray. Within the mangrove forest, the waters were very placid and clear, allowing us to see what was present under the surface of the water

In the morning, we made a landing at Bahia Urbina, which is a place where the coast has a lava-rock outcropping and a black-sand beach. On the hiking trail, we saw many tortoises and land iguanas. There were quite a few poison apple trees, incense trees, and muyuyo. The poison apple is named in Spanish *manzanillo* (*Hippomane mancinella*, family *Euphorbiaceae*)[37]. It is a tree that produces a milky sap, like many other euphorbes, and the iguanas eat the berries, as their digestive systems are able to handle the poisonous compounds. (Note: They are not related to the true apple trees.) There is an invasive grass, elephant grass (*Pennisetum purpureum*, family *Poaceae*)[38] on the Galapagos Islands. It is related to two invasive species in Arizona: buffelgrass (*Pennisetum setaseum*)[39] and fountaingrass (*Pennisetum ciliare*)[40]. We also saw the thin-leafed Darwin's shrub (*Darwiniothamnus tenuifolius*, family *Asteraceae*).[41] In the afternoon, we sailed to Punta Moreno, where we did a hike. It has a view of three volcanoes: Isabela's Sierra Negra and Cerro Azul and Fernandina's La Cumbre. Along the trail over pahoehoe lava rock, we stopped at several lagoons, where we saw ducks and other birds. The three cacti, which are the lava cactus, candelabra, and prickly pear, were present on the lava rock. Along the coast, we were able to see more penguins, lots of marine iguanas, cormorants, and blue-footed boobies.

We arrived at Isla Floreana at Punta Cormorant, where we hiked to a lagoon that had flamingos. They could be seen in the distance, fishing for brine shrimp and flying overhead at times. There were also some stilts present. There were also some more species of plants to be seen, such as mesquite (*Prosopis juliflora*, family *Fabaceae*),[42] paloverde (*Parkinsonia aculeata*, family *Fabaceae*)[43] and several asterids. We also sailed to Isla Champion, where we saw several tropic birds, finches, a mockingbird, sea lions, and an interesting geologic formation inside a crater, forming a small bay into the island. After lunch, we sailed to Post Office Bay, where there is an old mailbox where people "mail" postcards. Basically, this works on an honor system in which someone places a postcard into the mailbox. Then another traveler will pick up the postcard and hand deliver it to the intended recipient. In the afternoon, we went to Black Beach and then headed to the islands, where we went into a tortoise enclosure. There were some endemic medium ground finches (*Geospiza fortis*),[44] warblers, an owl, and other species of birds. In addition, there were also many species of plants that grow only in this part of the world, as well as lichen. The forest was very lush, being at a higher elevation above sea level. We also stopped at several of the pirate caves and a site that had a moai carving. It was a very small version of those found on Rapa Nui. The end of the day was a visit to the Hotel Wittmer, where we were able to take a rest and view some of the historic information presented, as if being in a museum. I purchased the book *Floreana*, which is a history of the human habitation of Floreana from the point of view of the Wittmer family, from the gift shop.

We arrived at Puerto Ayora on Isla Santa Cruz, which is the economic and scientific heart of the Galapagos. In the morning, we went to the Charles Darwin Research Station, which had enclosures for raising the various species of tortoises for the different islands with the intention of releasing them. There were various research facilities. Plus, there was a museum presenting a comprehensive overview of the natural history of the islands. Afterward, we took a trip to the highlands, where we traversed the seven different vegetative zones that exist in the Galapagos at different elevation levels. There was a park where we saw lots of tortoises and finches. Of particular interest was the woodpecker finch, not present on the other islands. In addition, we saw several rails, which is a duck-like bird, and other species of birds. From there, we hiked into a lava tube and then visited Los Gemelos, which are enormous pit craters. There were also a lot of interesting plants that included the imported quinine, which has become invasive also. The day ended with a return to Puerto Ayora, where we saw several sea lions sleeping on the benches on the pier. Interestingly, one of the sea lions was snoring and in a state of REM sleep. It makes me wonder what those creatures are dreaming about.

After arriving at Isla Española, we went on a hike to Punta Suarez, which is a birder's paradise. We saw albatross, blue-footed boobies, Galapagos hawks, finches, and many colorful marine iguanas. A grand opportunity arose as we were sailing to Gardner Bay. We had an opportunity to see some humpback whales as they were surfacing in one of the bays near a beach. I went kayaking again, during which I was viewing closely the interesting volcanic geologic formations. Afterward, we did a walk along a sandy beach where we saw sea turtles along the beach, finches, a couple of Hood mockingbirds, and some golden rays.

We arrived at Isla San Cristobal, which is the easternmost island and geologically the oldest. We saw many geologic formations, red-footed boobies, mockingbirds, tropic birds, swallow-tailed gulls, and lava lizards. At Punta Pitt, we did a really nice hike, allowing us to see the different views of the rock formations, peaks, and ocean. In the afternoon, we went to Cerro Brujo, where I did more kayaking. This geological feature is an eroded tuff cone, and it was one of the places visited by Charles Darwin. There is a white coralline sand beach, which we hiked on. Behind the beach is a lagoon that is home to pelicans, blue-footed boobies, flycatchers, swallow-tailed gulls, and the Chatham mockingbird. We sailed at sunset to Kicker Rock, which is an eroded tuff cone that rises about 500 feet above the sea. It became very photogenic as the light from the setting sun created some beautiful effects on the contours of the cliffs.

We went on a boat ride at Mosquera Island, which is actually a narrow sandpit with a large population of sea lions. The geologic features were interesting because an uplift occurred, raising the features. In the afternoon, back on Isla Santa Cruz, we went to Turtle Cove, exploring the mangrove coves and inlets. We saw green sea turtles mating, several whitetip reef sharks, and several rays. This was a very scenic area, consisting of white mangroves (*Laguncularia racemose*, family *Combretaceae*)[45] and red mangroves (*Rhizophora mangle*, family *Rhrizophoraceae*)[46].

We had an early start to Sombrero Chino, which is an example of the volcanic origins of the Galapagos. There are many lava formations and lava tubes. We saw several sea lions nursing. Also, there were lots of pelicans and frigate birds. During the latter part of the morning, I went kayaking, and I was able to see more sea lions swimming. Since the waters were very clear, I was able to see in certain locations fish of various species and colors. In the afternoon, I went snorkeling and saw many species of fish of various sizes and all colors. At Isla Rabida, we started a hike at one of the red sand beaches to a large lagoon, where we saw more flamingos. This is also a very scenic place; the red sand is attributed to the red-colored rock—due to oxidation—being eroded away by the sea. The lagoon contains brackish water for the flamingos and other species of birds, such as mockingbirds. Hiking on the higher elevations, we saw more Palo Santo trees, cacti, and crotons, and some tomato plants. The views of the coast, with its red sand rocks, were spectacular. A good way to end the day!

When we arrived at Isla Bartolomé, we did a nice hike on a wooden walkway, which was constructed to prevent erosion of the volcanic rock by tourists. This island was the result of some violent lava and ash activity in the past. It possessed many interesting geologic features, which included lava tubes, ah-ah rock formations, spatter cones, cinder cones, and tuff formations. There were some locations where pioneering plants such as lava cactus grew. We saw lots of pelicans, a hawk, and one or two rays. In the afternoon, we returned to Isla Santiago, stopping at Sullivan Bay, which presents a recently formed lava field. There are interesting pahoehoe formations in all shapes, forms, and sizes. We saw several plant species attempting to grow in various spots on the lava field, such as lava cactus, some *Scalesia*, and *Mollugo* (*Mollugo flavescens*, family *Mulluginaceae*)[47].

We arrived at Isla Santa Fe, which is home to a unique species of land iguana. We saw several. There is a forest of a species of giant prickly pear cactus that have adapted for protection against the land iguanas. We saw several hawks, with one standing on top of a national park monument, presenting an excellent photo opportunity. Although the rice rat, which arrived here without human intervention, is present, we did not see any. In the afternoon, we arrived at South Plaza Island, which is also a geologically uplifted island. It is covered with red sesuvium and prickly pear cacti, which serve as a good food source for the land iguanas, and we saw quite a few of those. We did a loop hike on the island, where we saw land iguanas, sea lions, tropic birds, swallow-tailed gulls, and frigate birds.

On the last day, back on Isla Santa Cruz, we visited Playa Las Bachas, which has two white sand beaches and a small brackish lagoon. On the rocky lava outcrops, we saw pelicans. We also saw more marine iguanas, lava lizards, mockingbirds, and more interesting plants. After this morning excursion, we boarded the plane to Quito, where we spent the last night of this trip.

As I spend much time in the natural world, I feel connected to the larger ecosystem of the planet Earth and Nature. I enjoy the outdoors! On many of my hikes, I see the animals approach me, and they seem curious about my presence. Animals are *not* stupid! I recall one of the fundamentalist Christians approaching me stating that animals are just dumb blobs. Rubbish! I feel that I have a connection with the animals. I even have a connection with the plants and the minerals of this planet.

Going back very far in time as our solar system formed, our sun, planets, asteroids, Kuiper Belt objects, and Oort cloud objects coalesced. It was quite a process, being part of a larger cosmic evolution. Our planet Earth came to exist as a result. Ultimately, our Earth, along with humans, animals, plants, and minerals, formed from stardust. This means that there is a connection with the cosmos. In turn, I have a connection with the other living creatures of the Earth.

The human species has developed technologies that have allowed it to continue to explore space. Most have been in the form of probes, which are sent to various planets, moons, asteroids, and the edge of the solar system. Men have been to the moon and back. With the International Space Station, there is heavy traffic of people going back and forth above the Earth's atmosphere.

Much of it is good, and it is good that there is scientific curiosity to understand what is out there in the universe; hence, this is why our educational system needs to be improved to have our young people be inspired by science.

I have had the opportunity to speak to a couple of people who are astronauts. Harrison Schmidt shared with me some of his experiences, and he did mention that the radiation in interplanetary space is a hazard that will have to be dealt with. He also conveyed his experience with the ultra-fine dust on the Moon's surface. When it was unintentionally carried into the lunar module, it spread around the cabin. It was quite an uncomfortable experience to inhale it.

Another astronaut, Richard "Mike" Mullane, was aboard the International Space Station. He told me about his experiences of looking down onto the Earth's landmasses and oceans, expressing that, at present, this is the only home we have, and we have to take care of it. He also mentioned how silent space was inside the space station, with the exception of some computer system or other equipment running. There were *no* sounds of nature!

On a PBS documentary, I watched an interview with an astronaut, and he mentioned that, while being out on the space station, he missed many things on Earth. What he said caught my attention, as he mentioned that he missed hearing the sounds of the birds and feeling the wind. I thought about what he mentioned, as I am constantly hiking, and I enjoy listening to the birds sing or the wind blow.

Having traveled the world myself, I have come to realize two things: how big the Earth is and how small the Earth is. The astronauts are correct that this planet is the only planet that we have as home. How ready is the human species to actually settle the Moon and then the planet Mars? Barack Obama and Donald Trump have said a few things about a manned mission to Mars. In some ways, it is a noble idea, similar to John F. Kennedy's idea of getting humans to the Moon. We arrived there in 1969; however, we have not returned there since 1973.

We would have to return to the Moon again. This would help us to become established on the Moon. The Moon may serve as a launchpad, allowing us to proceed to Mars. Meanwhile, as I see how humanity is trashing the Earth, with anthropogenically caused climate change being just a small part of the larger picture, I ask: Are we going to trash the Moon and Mars?

One of the things that really bothers me is the manner in which we just toss away our rubbish, creating landfills, which truly have their own actual and potential hazards. In reality, they are ticking time bombs! They also produce methane, which is another greenhouse gas. In some cases, the methane is being siphoned off to be used as fuel. Unfortunately, many people discard all types of waste into the regular trash, including hazardous chemical waste. This collects in liquids, called leachate. Meanwhile, people think: out of sight, out of mind. This will come back to haunt us!

If we are to venture out into space and colonize other planets and moons, then we will really need to get a handle on what we do on Earth. Although we are making some progress regarding recycling, unfortunately it is still something of a joke. Metals, which can be easily recycled, are simply discarded in the regular waste stream. It takes only 25 percent of the energy to melt down a metal and fabricate it into a new product compared to extracting it from ore. If we are going to settle other worlds, we cannot just discard our trash onto their surfaces.

Think of our oceans! Now, we have gyres of plastic floating on the surfaces of Earth's oceans. We need to clean that mess up. This plastic is eaten by marine wildlife. Often, the plastic becomes stuck in the digestive systems of a marine animal, killing it. The ultraviolet radiation from the sun causes plastic to degrade as long-chained polymers are snipped to shorter molecules. This process causes the release of toxic compounds that are present in plastics. Such compounds, along with pesticides, polychlorinated biphenyls (PCBs), and other polychlorinated hydrocarbons then enter the food chain.

Chapter 5

AN INCAPACITATED EDUCATIONAL SYSTEM

"A balanced mind is necessary to balance
the unbalanced minds of others."
—U Ba Khin

Here is another fact about Donald Trump, which I find to be very ludicrous. He does *not* read any books. In my opinion, if a person wishes to be the president of the United States, such a person should have an intellectual curiosity. For all of President Bill Clinton's faults, he did possess an intellectual curiosity. Donald Trump has *no* intellectual curiosity—whatsoever!

Perhaps a comparison can be made between Donald Trump and George W. Bush. What these two people have in common is limited intellect. In the case of George W. Bush, he posseses weak intellectual faculties that was obvious in his expression of the English language—the manner in which he constructed his sentences with his very bad grammar. He did read books; however, it is doubtful that he retained much of the information that he read.

Donald Trump, on the other hand, is not lacking in intelligence; however, he chooses to remain ignorant. He prides himself on not reading any books. He chooses to not learn anything new. The result is that he will remain ignorant of many subject matters. He is ignorant about history. He is *very* ignorant about science!

Both Donald Trump and George W. Bush lack knowledge of the history of the Middle East. Without that knowledge base, a big blunder was made by invading Iraq. With Donald Trump, the situation in the Middle East was something he inherited, like his predecessor, Barack Obama. The problem was that, with his lack of understanding of basic facts, there was *no* coherent Middle East policy. If anything, the intelligence services such as the NSA and CIA had an understanding of who and what organizations were operating in the Middle East and around the world. Instead, Donald Trump chose to ignore what was presented to him. He thought that he knew more than the people in the intelligence agencies knew.

The world has known many rises and falls! Many empires throughout history have come and gone. This is true, whether one is speaking about the Roman Empire, the Persian Empire, the Khmer Empire, the Han, Tang, and Ming dynasties in China, or any other empires and kingdoms throughout history. This is all part of *human* history, in contrast to the natural history of the planet.

The natural processes at work are governed by the laws of physics and chemistry, whereby evolutionary processes are at work as an expression of the underlying physical and chemical processes. Through astrophysical processes, there was a cosmic evolution through which our galaxy and, in turn, our solar system were formed. Through biophysical and biochemical processes, life emerged. This was a step-by-step process, starting from simpler molecules to molecules of greater complexity. Eventually, some of those molecules were able to replicate and/or become the templates for the construction of other molecules. All living creatures, including the human species, are products of this evolutionary process.

History involves the study of human social institutions from prehistory to the present. There are different episodes of history, whether one is speaking about classical or ancient history, medieval history, the Renaissance, the Reformation, the Enlightenment era, or the modern era. There is military history, the history of science, the history of music, the history of art, and the history of philosophy.

One of the things I do prior to embarking on my trips is to do some research on the history of the places that I wish to visit. This helps me to understand better how what I encounter in any particular region or country fits into its historical context. It is also to some degree an iterative process, as I continue to learn more while traveling. Often, what I learn during one trip helps me in planning my next trip.

It is very disheartening to realize that many of our elected officials fail to learn from history. In fact, this is not only true of people in high places. There are just so many people who do not even know basic geography. There is a gap somewhere, and this is something that is difficult to understand. The result is that people have a snapshot view of an event, whether it is presented on the news or heard about through some other means. It is seldom questioned how we arrived at this point.

Take any event, including climate change and a war in the Middle East, and it must be understood in its larger context.

At fault is an educational system that fails to teach, leaving a large segment of the population lacking in knowing what they need to know, which applies to our elected officials, and is part of the problem of why we had Donald Trump in office, a man who had *no* understanding of science and little understanding of history. As a consequence, we had a president who effected policies that were ambivalent in the Middle East and potentially destructive to the environment.

Quite a while ago, I arrived at the conclusion that there is a strong anti-intellectual movement in the United States. That is reflected in the media in general. It seems that younger children are curious about the world; however, something seems to happen to most children as they become older, and they lose that curiosity. Religious institutions frequently force people—especially the young—to *not* question the religious dogma of the church, for one example.

Another example is the very negative influence of television programming. Over the decades, I have become very critical of the commercial television stations such as ABC, CBS, and NBC. Of course, with all of the cable television stations, there is much more to be critical of. Personally, I have made my decision to only watch PBS. I do obtain some additional news through several international internet news sites. Most of the other television programming, with the exception of sports, is just plain rubbish! We have a lot of thirty-second sound bites, which are now even down to ten seconds or less! There is just so much out there that is very imbecile, stupid, and nonsensical. In addition, all the sex and violence do nothing to enhance any person's values in any way. I will just be very blunt. Most of the television programming is just plain bullshit!

What is the need for all of this violence? How does any of that enrich or edify a person? Is it all geared to make people think a certain way? Here is an excerpt from a book that was written by the Dalai Lama and translated into German:

Denken Sie einen Augenblick an das Problem der Gewalt,
ein Aspekt der Welt, der offenbar immer mehr, Anlaß
zur Besorgnis gibt. Es ist etwas Gefährliches, Unheilvol-

les. Ob im Fernsehen oder im Kino – nach dem wenigen zu schließen, das ich auf meinen Reisen in verschiedene westliche Länder zu sehen bekam—hat man den Eindruck daß es nur Häßlichkeit, Gewalt, Brutalität, und Sitten-losigkeit gibt. Es ist zugleich eine Aggression und eine Regression. Es sind vollig sinn- und gefühllose Morde und Blutbäder. Toten um des Tötens willen nichts weiter. Glauben Sie, daß das keinen Einfluß auf die Seele hat? Alles wird letztlich farblos und abgeschmackt, die Welt verliert ihre Konturen und damit ihre Schönheit.[1]

The author's translation from German into English is as follows: Think for a moment about the problem of violence, an aspect of the world that seems to be a growing concern. It is something dangerous, ominous. Whether on television or in the theater—judging from the little that I have seen on my travels to various Western countries—one gets the impression that there is nothing but ugliness, violence, brutality, and immorality. It is an aggression and a regression at the same time. There exist completely senseless and callous murders and bloodbaths. Killing for the sake of killing—nothing more. Would you think that this has no effect on the soul? In the end everything becomes colorless and tasteless, the world loses its contours and with it its beauty.

Does not this type of programming only dumb a nation down? Of course! Especially among the young people, seeing violence and stupidity can only have a negative effect on the psyche. It is what they see and learn from viewing television that penetrates into the depths of the subconscious mind.

The subconscious mind is very tricky in that it doesn't discrim-inate in the same manner as the conscious mind. It is like a sponge that absorbs scenes and words that become embedded in the psyche. Over the years, I have come to avoid this type of content.

I do not want to see it! I do not want to hear it! By watching programming of a more scientific or historical nature, I am not only benefiting my intellect. I am also feeding my subconscious mind something more positive.

At times, I need to stop at a store, such as Best Buy, and I walk through the aisles. I notice the section where they have the video games. I think, *Why is it that there is such a thirst for those types of video games in which one blows up other people or objects? Where is the sense in that?* Certainly, when people play those video games, such actions are permeating their subconscious minds. I am thinking back to those shooting incidents at so many venues around the United States, including schools. Whenever I hear or read another news report about a mass shooting, I question whether those people were involved with repeatedly playing violent video games. It seems as if they are acting out what they see while playing video games, except that it becomes real life. The outcomes are tragic!

This is something that I also see as part of the larger anti-intellectual movement. It is another way that one can waste one's life away. Just sitting in front of a television or playing video games all day is just plain wasting time instead of being more productive in society. We have reached a low common denominator of programming and presentations on pseudoscience and superstition that are most definitely a kind of celebration of ignorance.

Once again, I have to comment on how our elected officials, including Donald Trump, get into the mix of debates regarding gun control whenever there is a mass shooting. It seems that, regardless of what side one is on, there is a deeper issue that is missed. What is at the heart of the mind or psyche involved with those acts of violence performed by the perpetrators?

Observing Donald Trump, I see in him a person who has a big ego. I ask the question of how he became president of the United States. I realize that one must consider the present political circumstances, along with his past. Even though he has acquired great wealth, it was not sufficient for him. He needed to obtain power, and, seeing that Barack Obama was a lame-duck president, he seized the opportunity. He succeeded! Was his ego satisfied? Up to a point.

What he essentially started to do was seek out ways to undo many of the policies of Barack Obama. Where there was a dysfunctional system that involved quite a lot of vitriol and acrimony, it only intensified. Even though Donald Trump appointed people into his cabinet to support him with his own agenda—as many of them had connections to the coal, oil, and gas industries—the situation in the White House remained chaotic during his administration. After the 2016 election, prior to President Joe Biden's administration, the White House staff turnover was phenomenal. How could one keep up with who was coming and going? It was a revolving door. It was a ludicrous situation! President Biden's administration has been more organized and stable.

And the corruption in the Trump administration was abysmal! Many of Trump's staff, managers, and attorneys have found themselves in a lot of trouble. Even now, when I watch *Deutsche Welle*, *BBC News*, or the *PBS NewsHour*, I learn about the turbulent activity and the people surrounding Donald Trump. What a mess!

One of the things that transpired during the 2016 election campaign that got Donald Trump elected was his constant conflicts with people of all types, including the religious. It was comical to watch the interaction between him and the pope. Other conflicts involved his lawsuits. Once he became president, nothing changed, or, if anything did change, the list of individuals he was in conflict with only grew.

No doubt, not all of the problems, such as the political conflicts in the Middle East, inflation, and poverty, can be attributed to Donald Trump, per se, as he inherited many. No doubt, our US Congress, likewise, is dysfunctional because there is a great amount of dissension there also. Most of that dissension and acrimony is between Republicans and Democrats. There are times, too, when there is dissension within the political parties. Most of the time, things become stonewalled, and our Congress becomes a do-nothing Congress.

Of the issues discussed—whether they are tax plans, the Affordable Care Act, the environment, immigration, gun control, or a myriad of other issues—one of the most important issues is the national debt. It is seldom mentioned! Although I had some misgivings about Al Gore, he was right about two issues: the national debt and the environment.

These are the two issues that the Republicans, including Donald Trump, have tossed under the bus. When Barack Obama was president, the Republicans complained vehemently about spending. Then, during his presidential campaign, Donald Trump proffered up his version of a tax plan, which would decrease corporate taxes, reduce taxes on the wealthy, and increase the budget deficit. Woohoo! Why are Republicans not complaining *now* about the budget deficits? Have those bums in Washington—including Donald Trump—missed something again? The national debt is the summation of *all* budget deficits that go back in time into the early nineteenth century. In addition, we have a situation in which some awesome technological powers are in the hands of a very few, and few representing the public interest can even grasp the issues.

I believe that there is more happening in Washington than what they are disclosing to the public. Over a decade ago, there was a book written by Gerald J. Swanson, who is a professor of economics at the University of Arizona. Its title is *America the Broke*. I purchased a copy of his book and attended his book signing. It was very revealing. All I can say is that people better wake up. Wake up, America!

As I have mentioned above, anti-intellectualism is strong

within the United States. The educational systems of many states have deteriorated. During the financial crisis of 2008 and 2009, many states encountered financial problems. This had the effect of cutting back on funding at all levels, which meant kindergarten to twelfth-grade education. Also, the state universities were affected. Teachers that were teaching grade school and high school were stuck in low-paying jobs. They were not given the respect that they deserved. They were under great stress. They even had to pay out of their own pockets to purchase school supplies for their students. I am asking, What on Earth is going on?

At the university level, tuition has increased far more rapidly than the rate of inflation. This forces students to take out ever more burdensome student loans to get an education. It also means, in turn, that students will be saddled with debt long after they are no longer students. What ever happened to the concept that state university education should be as free as possible?

This is a sign that many of the people in government for those states do *not* have their priorities straight. There seem to be fewer people interested in science. Here and there are attempts to get people interested in science, technology, engineering, and math (STEM). That is good; however, more financial backing would help greatly.

What is fundamentally important? The educational system needs to be supported in such a manner that it is treated as an investment in the students. This means that education at state institutions should be free. The situation is different for private universities, if students choose to enroll there, where qualifying scholarships can be awarded for academic performance. Teachers at the grade school and high school levels should be given higher wages, treated as professionals, and treated with greater respect. Of course, also essential, teachers should collaborate with the parents.

Regarding the curricula, a certain emphasis must be placed

on reading, writing, and arithmetic. Importantly, greater emphasis should be placed upon science, geography, and history. When I meet so many people who do not know basic history, it leaves me wondering, what are they teaching these days in grade school? Or in high school? Also, what training do the teachers have to teach? If a student doesn't know where Iraq is on a map, something definitely is *wrong*!

There also needs to be an investment at the national level. With a US Congress that seems so dysfunctional, I ask the question: What is the federal government doing to invest more in education? I simply do not know! It almost appears that they are allowing a dumbing down of America to occur. Neil deGrasse Tyson, who is an astrophysicist and director of the Hayden Planetarium in New York City, made a statement saying that if we do not have a scientifically literate public, then the amount of science done in the United States will decrease. This will cause the United States to fall behind other nations. He also said that if other countries such as Germany or China are engaged in scientific research, he'll at least be happy that others in the world are doing science.

With the television media presenting all of that rubbish, it is also a distraction from getting people interested in science or other intellectual pursuits. It is also true that people have now even become addicted to their cell phones and social media. The tendency is for people to become distracted by the internet, where many sites present a lot of their own junk.

I believe that the internet is a good resource for hiking, backpacking, and travel information; however, there I let the internet serve me. I do *not* let it enslave me! I do like to download historic documentaries from YouTube, but, at the same time, I am aware that there is a lot of pseudoscience presented. Some of the conspiracy theories out there reflect some real lunacy. Frequently, I even wonder if people who only obtain their sources of information from selected internet sites of a certain genre will then end up having a limited understanding of the world.

Perhaps people who visit only certain sites will be open only to certain ideas and close their minds to other ideas, which would be very limiting. I find that, even if I don't agree with a political ideology or religious view, I still want to understand something about it. As an example, I read the *Communist Manifesto* even though I am not a communist. I do not agree with that ideology; however, because I am intellectually curious, I want to know more about communism. This is true for me about many topics.

I mentioned how the national debt has increased to such a level that we are now at more than $30 trillion in debt, and it is continuing to grow. It is an abomination that we are leaving our children and grandchildren with this debt. Here, I do wish I knew more about the details of how the national debt is being financed; however, certain things are clear to me.

A good portion of this debt is attributed to the wars in Iraq and Afghanistan. We will be dealing with the consequences of those wars for a long time to come. What is often overlooked is that interest will need to be paid on this debt. This interest money could be better used elsewhere. With our educational system in a state of distress, doesn't it make sense to have that money go as an investment in education instead? Instead of having wasted that money on those wars, wouldn't it have been better to invest that money in environmental cleanup, renewable energy, education, and infrastructure instead?

Somehow, I think that the US Congress needs to wake up! Its members are in public office to satisfy their own agendas, and it seems like they have forgotten many of the real issues. Those real issues are, in reality, the issues of the people. Issues that pertain to better foreign relations should take precedence over just being trigger happy and ready for war.

Let's discuss religion. Is Donald Trump a religious person? I do *not* know. Whatever relationship he has with God is his own affair. It is *not* my concern. What has troubled me for some time is the pushiness of so many religious people. They want to convert others to their religion because they think that only they possess the truth. Nonsense!

With Donald Trump, I only question his religion because of his behavior. As I have encountered many religious people who profess to be Christian yet exhibit behavior contrary to what Jesus the Messiah presented, I have found them to be hypocritical. During George W. Bush's administration, we would constantly hear about his religious faith. Fine. Since the principle of separation of church and state is in the US Constitution, please don't bring religion into the public arena. The United States is *not* a theocracy. It is a republic!

Often, there are those who promote religious dogma—even in our educational system. An example is the debate between those who believe in evolution versus those who believe in creationism.

Evolution, which I discussed a little earlier in this chapter, is the process by which different kinds of living organisms developed and diversified from earlier forms of life during the history of the Earth. The theory of evolution purports that life on earth evolved from some universal common ancestor about 3.8 billion years ago. It is a theory in the scientific sense of the word. This means that it is supported by an overwhelming amount of evidence and accepted as a collection of facts by the scientific community. Scientific methods have been utilized in the disciplines of biology, astronomy, geology, paleontology, molecular biology, genomics, physics, and biophysics to present these vast bodies of evidence for deep time (billions of years), which is the temporal context for allowing evolution to occur through natural processes.

Creationism, which is also called intelligent design, is the belief that life and the universe were created by a supernatural being—that is, an "intelligent designer." Many creationists believe that the universe is only six to ten thousand years old. They also have their science called creationism. Since 1929, the term "creationism" in the United States has been associated with Christian fundamentalism and specifically with a disbelief in evolution and a belief in a young Earth. In actuality, creationism is *not* supported by evidence, as this is basically religious dogma that is based upon literal interpretation of the Bible. I regard it as pseudoscience. Besides, astrophysicists have determined that the age of the universe is approximately 13.8 billion years old since the big bang marking its beginning. A god who creates the universe in seven literal days and gives it the appearance of being 13.8 billion years old is a very deceptive god. A deceptive god of this sort is certainly *not* worthy of any praise—much less worship!

The popular media often portrays the creation versus evolution debate as science versus religion, with creation being religious and evolution being scientific. It happens that there are many Christians and people of other religions who accept the scientific principles of evolution. There are many Christians who are also scientists whom I have met, and they do *not* interpret everything in the Bible literally. I met a grade-school teacher who has a background in marine biology, and I had a conversation about evolution with her because I was curious about what they were permitted to teach in the classroom. She told me that she teaches evolution as it pertains to her field of marine biology. In fact, she taught me some new facts about the evolution of corals, which is new information since I studied biology about three decades earlier. She expressed to me that she is a Christian, and she does not see any conflict. Her words were: "Evolution is how it happened. God is who did it."

If only our elected officials would think more logically like her! Instead, just like everything else, the teaching of evolution has become so politicized.

I have nothing against Christianity; however, we live in a nation—and a world—where there are many religions. Also, there are people like me who choose to not be affiliated. I follow Eastern philosophies instead. Then there are others who are atheists or have no religion. My philosophy is to live and let live!

Chapter 6

DANGERS OF JUNK SCIENCE

"Nature has always been my friend, my mentor, and my muse."
—Karen K. Schaefer

Another attribute of the supporters of Donald Trump was their position regarding climate science. They didn't accept the findings of the climate scientists, or they even considered global warming a fraud. Here again, I think that they accepted some nonsensical conspiracy theories, which they found on YouTube or some other medium. There is a lot of pseudoscience and pseudohistory present on the internet.

Several trips that I have made have been into the northwest United States and Canada. Glacier National Park was high on my list to visit; therefore, I traveled through parts of Montana and several national parks in Canada.

One of the things that I have learned is how the glaciers are and have been shrinking in size over the decades. In Glacier National Park in Montana and Kootenay, Jasper, Banff, and Waterton Lakes National Parks in Canada, it was obvious how the ice was melting. The glaciers are shrinking because more ice is melting than is being added through precipitation.

I recall one of my trips up to Glacier National Park in Montana.

After driving up the Continental Divide, I parked along the side of the road, appreciating the view from high above. It was a glorious sight to the west—and to the east! Of course, the mountain goats, having no fear of me, were also right nearby. I continued to go west, which was downhill. It was slow, especially at certain turns. When I was close to Lake McDonald, I decided to go on a hike. That hike was a walk into the essence of Glacier National Park. It was a hike into a pristine forest, carpeted by fallen timbers, branches, ferns, and mosses. Green was to be found everywhere, except, when looking straight up, the clear blue sky was seen. In fact, Montana is known as the Big Sky State. Water, ice, and jagged peaks were to be seen in the distance. It was a place where the powers that raised the mountains were at work. It was also the place where the powers tearing the mountains down were at work. Streams, rivers, and creeks could be seen and had to be crossed. Frequently, I would observe the cascading waterfalls from the melting snow flow into glacial lakes. The lakes were most beautiful, enhanced by their turquoise green color, which could be attributed to the suspended microscopic particles of mineral particles that had been ground from the action of the glaciers. The glaciers themselves were at work, eroding the mountains into jagged peaks and serrated ridges. The blooms of an assortment of flowers of various species further enhanced the beauty of the landscapes.

Naturally, during the Pleistocene Epoch, there were many episodes of expansion and retreat of the continental ice sheets. This was also the time of the Pleistocene megafauna. This is certainly attributed to the natural cycles of precession, the eccentricity of the Earth's orbit, the degree of tilt of the Earth's axis, and the geologic activities of the Earth. Presently, the inclination of the Earth's tilt is approximately 23.5 degrees. All of these phenomena have contributed to the changing climate of the Earth.

Now that the human population has greatly expanded through-out the Earth, we are living in the Anthropocene Epoch. From the Pleistocene, we went into the Holocene, and then into the Anthro-pocene. The Anthropocene began during the time of the Industrial Revolution, which was approximately 1760 CE. Now, we have human activities superimposed upon those natural phenomena.

The Industrial Revolution was the time when the consump-tion of fossil fuels increased greatly. As the human population grew, the amount of fossil fuel that was used increased even more. This consumption has resulted in the increase of carbon dioxide (CO_2) emissions into the atmosphere. Carbon dioxide *is* a greenhouse gas!

The rate of increase in fossil fuel consumption increased again enormously after World War II. With the changes in the United States economy after that war, there was a sense of prosperity. Meanwhile Europe was still recovering from the devastation of war. This contributed to the rate of increase in consumption. With an economy based upon consumption, industry was built up to fab-ricate products of all sorts. With that came the demand for power; hence, the need to burn fossil fuels.

Presently, we have entered a new age of consumption, being in the digital age. This involves the need to consume more for manu-facturing, running, and maintaining our computer systems. This is especially true for powering the large server farms run by Google, Amazon, Microsoft, and many other corporations that are part of their infrastructures for their data archival and retrieval systems. Let's not forget one thing! Those server farms consume energy and produce a lot of heat. That heat energy, unless it can somehow be utilized, is wasted energy.

Of course, energy is required to run any business, government, or household. I likewise contribute to this consumption, as I am burning gasoline in my vehicle to get me to and from work and to my destinations on my road trips. I certainly do not forget that, when I am traveling internationally, I am in an airplane that is consuming jet fuel. All of those fuels utilized have their origin within the Earth. As these fuels are being burned, they are releasing CO_2. Of course, coal-fired power plants release other harmful byproducts, including nitrogen dioxide (NO_2) and sulfur dioxide (SO_2). Meanwhile, the ash, resulting from the burning of coal, can release its own toxic metals, including mercury, lead, and cadmium.

Now, having clarity on the fact that, since the Industrial Revolution, the amount of CO_2 has increased in the atmosphere, we see how the Earth's climate is changing as a consequence of human activities. Referring back to my trips to Jasper, Banff, and Kootenay National Parks, there are interpretive signs that display where the glaciers used to extend. Obviously, they have been shrinking. No doubt, there is evidence to support the fact that the shrinking glaciers are one of many effects of global warming.

There are many highly respectable scientists who work in geosciences, geophysics, hydrology, atmospheric science, climate science, meteorology, and ecology and are studying these phenomena. I have great respect for one of those scientists, Jonathan Overpeck, who is investigating this subject and has set up the Institute of the Environment at the University of Arizona. I attended several of his presentations and symposia and other lecture series. The bottom line is that now, in this Anthropocene Epoch, the human species is influencing the changes in climate in addition to the natural phenomena. In fact, the human contribution has actually been greater than that of the natural phenomena.

The science is out there. The scientific investigations and proofs are very clear; however, there is *strong* pushback. Many of the industries, such as coal, oil, gas, and mining, present their own science to refute the authentic science of people such as Jonathan Overpeck. Clearly, something is very wrong!

To take this a step further, many politicians do *not* buy into the scientific research of the climate scientists. Donald Trump, who is extremely ignorant about science in general and climate science in particular, is a climate-science denier.

I find it so hypocritical that people in public office and industry who deny the science to understand the phenomenon of the changing climate accept products that are inventions resulting from scientific and engineering principles. After all, our computers exist because many scientists contributed to understanding the scientific principles of solid-state physics, quantum theory, and other areas of physics, chemistry, and electrical engineering. With science, many principles and concepts are interconnected. This is very true for understanding weather and climate.

Then, there are those weather phenomena that are more extreme. For example, when there is a freezing-cold air mass, breaking off from the polar regions and moving south, this causes a sudden freezing over the eastern United States, even as far south as Florida. I recall some years back when a cold air mass, taking the form of a vortex as it appeared on a weather map, broke away from the Hudson Bay area in Canada. That package of cold air moved from Hudson Bay to North and South Dakota, then to Colorado, Wyoming, and Utah. Afterward, it moved farther south over Arizona and New Mexico. In fact, that air mass moved as far south as the states of Sonora, Chihuahua, Sinaloa, and Michoacán in Mexico before it started to warm up.

Yes, such extremes of cold do happen, and this is part of the pattern of climate change involving global warming. What does Donald Trump say? When such a cold mass of air passed through the eastern United States, in a very cynical and snarky manner, he said, "Oh! We certainly can use some of the 'global warming'!" Why is such a comment made? First, he is a climate-change denier. He does *not* accept what the scientists say about climate change.

Then, many of his constituents who helped him to get elected are lobbyists from the fossil-fuel industry. No doubt, the tone of that statement is also reflective of someone who expresses acrimony.

It is stupefying, in this age of technological advancement and science, that this disdain for scientific truth is expressed. How did we get to this point? What Donald Trump and many other elected officials express in their comments does not only go against scientific truth. It also goes against my experience. This is because, during my travels, I see natural phenomena as they occur. I not only see them happen, but I experience them. Glacial retreat is something I have seen. As an example, I have been twice to Glacier National Park. I have repeated some hikes as I returned to several of the glaciers, and I noticed the changes after six years. They shrank! This means that I have experienced those changes as I have observed the natural world.

There is a common denominator between both the Bush II and the Trump administrations. It is climate change, a victim of a virus of science denial that has come to infect almost the entire modern Republican establishment. This ideology is not, in reality, conservative. Many rational conservatives are very appalled by this behavior, although there are many who are not. Instead, this ideology is some mutant child of toddler narcissism. It is definitely characterized by intellectual sloth. As I have traveled the world, I observered the changes that are happening, which include the shrinking glaciers, the phenological changes, and the destruction of rainforests. Meanwhile, because I am interested in science, any reading of books and scientific journal articles, any lectures and symposiums I attend, and any scientists whom I correspond with reinforce what I observe.

During my first trip to Africa, I was visiting and exploring Kenya and Tanzania. Being an avid hiker, I decided to do the hike and climb up Mount Kilimanjaro, which is part of the greater rift in Africa. It is a dormant volcano, and the highest point, Uhuru Peak, is 5,895 meters (19,340 feet) above sea level. Even though that mountain is so close to the equator, it is so high in elevation above sea level that it possesses glaciers. This is a mountain that takes several days to ascend, acclimatizing each day.

The hike begins at the Kilimanjaro National Park headquarters in Tanzania. (There are also routes to the summit that begin in Kenya.) The first day is a hike up to Mandara Hut, which is about the elevation of Mount Lemmon in the Santa Catalina Mountains. This segment of the hike is through an African tropical rainforest, appearing as a skirt around the mountain. The second day is the hike from Mandara Hut to Horombo Hut, which has an elevation approximately that of Humphreys Peak in the San Francisco Peaks, north of Flagstaff, Arizona. I noticed the lobelia trees, which have distant relatives on other continents, including in the Sonoran Desert in Arizona.

Lobelia deckenii is a species of flowering plant in the family *Campanulaceae*. It is a giant lobelia endemic to the mountains of Tanzania. It is listed as a threatened plant of the forests of Cherangani Hills, Kenya. It grows in moist areas, such as valley bottoms and moorland, in contrast to *Lobelia telekii* which grows in a similar but drier habitat. These two species produce occasional hybrids. *Lobelia deckenii* plants usually produce multiple rosettes. Each rosette grows for several decades, produces a single large inflorescence and hundreds of thousands of seeds, then dies. Because individual plants have multiple rosettes, they survive to reproduce repeatedly, and plants with more rosettes flower more frequently. It is iteroparous.

Lobelia deckenii plants usually form between one and eighteen rosettes which are connected underground. The individual rosettes grow slowly in the alpine environment and may take decades to reach reproductive size. The rosette that produces an inflorescence dies after flowering, but the remaining connected rosettes live on.

Lobelia deckenii is the only alpine species of lobelia that is native to Kilimanjaro, occurring between 3,800 and 4,300 meters (12,500 and 14,100 feet).[1]

As one approaches the hut, the vegetation becomes sparser. The third day involves a hike from Horombo Hut to Kibo Hut, which has an elevation similar to Mont Blanc in the Alps. At that elevation, the vegetation is extremely sparse, and patches of snow are present. The fourth day is when the ascent is made from Kibo Hut to Gilman's Point. In my case, I continued higher to Uhuru Peak. What a view! One could see, as I was counting, about seven different layers of clouds, where the clouds in the different layers were moving in different directions. Being at the summit, I could actually look inside the volcanic crater. This part of the trek was over snow and glaciers, as the crater rim of Kilimanjaro is surrounded by glaciers.

Being one who has a deep interest in natural history, I watch a lot of documentaries and programs such as *Nature*, National Geographic shows, and *NOVA*. There is always something to be learned by watching such programs, even if one is already very educated in science. Often it is scientific information outside of my field of science.

One of the documentaries explained climate science and how climate change is affecting Africa, including Mount Kilimanjaro. The glaciers there are also shrinking! Importantly, such changes are affecting the larger ecology of the peak and surrounding land areas, which, in turn, is part of the larger Serengeti. The glaciers are the sources of water for that surrounding tropical rainforest, and it is the source of water for the existing human development. When the glaciers of Mount Kilimanjaro melt away, where will the people obtain their water? On the National Center for Biotechnology

Information (NCBI) website, there is an article entitled "Glacier loss on Kilimanjaro continues unabated." These are the statistics that are presented:

The dramatic loss of Kilimanjaro's ice cover has attracted global attention. The three remaining ice fields on the plateau and the slopes are both shrinking laterally and rapidly thinning. Summit ice cover (areal extent) decreased approximately 1 percent per year from 1912 to 1953 and approximately 2.5 percent per year from 1989 to 2007. Of the ice cover present in 1912, 85 percent has disappeared and 26 percent of that present in 2000 is now gone. From 2000 to 2007, thinning (surface lowering) at the summits of the Northern and Southern Ice Fields was approximately 1.9 and 5.1 meters, respectively, which based on ice thicknesses at the summit drill sites in 2000 represents a thinning of approximately 3.6 percent and 24 percent, respectively. Furtwängler Glacier thinned approximately 50 percent at the drill site between 2000 and 2009. Ice volume changes (2000–2007) calculated for two ice fields reveal that nearly equivalent ice volumes are now being lost to thinning and lateral shrinking. The relative importance of different climatological drivers remains an area of active inquiry, yet several points bear consideration. Kilimanjaro's ice loss is contemporaneous with widespread glacier retreat in mid- to low latitudes. The Northern Ice Field has persisted at least 11,700 years and survived a widespread drought approximately 4,200 years ago that lasted approximately 300 years. We present additional evidence that the combination of processes driving the current shrinking and thinning of Kilimanjaro's ice fields is unique within an 11,700-year perspective. If current climatological conditions are sustained, the ice fields atop Kilimanjaro and on its flanks will likely disappear within several decades.[2]

The driest places on Earth are being affected by climate change. In addition, human activity is also affecting the wettest places on Earth. It is not only the forests surrounding Mount Kilimanjaro. It is all rainforests! I have seen the results of deforestation in Brazil, and I have also been to Southeast Asia, where I have seen similar areas that were deforested likewise and in other ways.

On a different trip to Asia, I traveled through Thailand, Cambodia, and Vietnam. Regarding that trip, passing through Cambodia, I was able to visit Angkor Wat, which is a collection of temple complexes as part of a supercomplex. This is also one of the places where there has been an episode of exploitation of resources. This was the capital of the Khmer Empire. It began in the eighth century under Jayavarman II and lasted until the thirteenth century. Similar to what was happening with the Mayan civilization several centuries earlier, the Khmer Empire had a system that exploited the resources of the land. There was deforestation of those lands during those centuries, likewise. Since the thirteenth century, until recently, the tropical rainforest has regenerated.

As I was visiting a museum in Ho Chi Minh City, I noticed the displays of grotesque fetuses in bottles of formaldehyde. Some had two heads, and others had all kinds of other deformities. These are the results of Agent Orange, Agent Blue, and other similar chemicals that were used as defoliants.

These defoliants also contributed a small component to deforestation. What is different about this, in contrast to the deforestation in Brazil or Indonesia, is that this involved war. In Brazil and Indonesia, land was cleared for agriculture. In Vietnam, the defoliants were used as weapons of war. Enter Monsanto! During the course of the Vietnam War, the US Department of Defense used Monsanto as their vendor for those defoliants.

Now, Monsanto has changed their business plan. One of their major products is Round Up, with the primary active chemical ingredient being glyphosate.[3] Monsanto has genetically modified corn and other food crops such that they are resistant to Round Up. Naturally, evolutionary processes are at work. As Round Up is being used to kill weeds, the corn and other crops that have been sprayed are surviving. The business plan for Monsanto is to sell Round Up *and* the genetically modified corn, which is now resistant to Round Up. This cannot last! This is because the weeds, such as pigweed, are also becoming resistant to the ingredient in Round Up—glyphosate. This is one example of many at work. (Similar processes are occurring at the molecular biological level to produce antibiotic-resistant bacteria.) This *is* evolution!

There is also a lot of junk science out there. With that, President Barack Obama was very conscientious with appointments to positions of scientific importance within his administration. There were people who actually knew what they were talking about. This was in complete contrast to his predecessor, George W. Bush. What was the case with George W. Bush is definitely true of Donald Trump. Donald Trump was following the junk science and going out of his way to select people who were completely unsuitable and unqualified for such posts. Donald Trump is ignorant about science, and he surrounded himself with people who were ignorant of science and ascribed to junk science. What all of these people have in common is that *none* of them are deep thinkers.

Chapter 7

WHY I AM A FREETHINKER

*"Never allow people who have given up on their dreams
to convince you to give up yours!"*
—Anonymous

When I am on my hikes out in the natural world, I often stop to listen to the sounds of nature and observe the animals. On almost every hike, I encounter wildlife, and I am very fortunate to have seen so much wherever I travel throughout the world. These animals that I encounter teach me many things, as I believe they have inner wisdom.

I have always been intrigued by the cat species that I have encountered. This includes some of the big cats, such as lions, leopards, cheetahs, and other species on my trips to Africa. Several times, I have encountered bobcats on my hikes in the Sonoran Desert. On one of the hikes, I saw some large paw prints from a mountain lion. Since they appeared quite fresh, the probability was very high that it saw me, but I did not see it. Cats tend to be very stealthy. They are intelligent creatures.

Another quality that I admire about cats is that they are very independent. One cannot herd cats. This is something that I also observe with house cats, and they also tend to have individual personalities.

I can relate to cats, and I seem to have similar qualities. I learned early in my life that I do not like being in crowds. Places where large groups of people collect together seem to make me feel very unsettled. One example is malls. I just don't like going to malls. Perhaps once or twice a year, when I need to go to one, I already have that short list of things in my mind that I need to purchase. I am quickly in, I obtain what I need, and, very quickly, I am out of there.

From a very early age, I was always interested in science. I read astronomy books. I read physics books. I also read books about biology, geology, and natural history. One of my fellow students in grade school told me: "You don't like to follow the crowd! You like to do your own thing instead." Very true! I had always been quiet. Sometimes they would make statements about me, such as, "He dances to a different drummer!"

When I was nine or ten years old, I already understood Einstein's theory of special relativity. When I was eleven, I understood general relativity. When I was thirteen or fourteen years old, I became intrigued by quantum theory. I was always extremely good at algebra, geometry, and mathematics. I knew that I liked science, and I wanted to be a scientist. In addition, I was also always interested in history. I wasn't only questioning the existence of the universe, the solar system, and the planet Earth. I was also asking questions about human origins and about ancient and modern civilizations.

An observation that I made is that there is almost nobody in my family who has the same interests I do. My father said that I should just go to a trade school and "be practical" and forget about all "that other stuff"! Fortunately, my inner compass told me to pursue my degrees in the sciences and engineering. There was only one other individual who ran against the grain of the family in manner of thinking. That was my one cousin, Richard, who, unfortunately, passed away in January 1994. That was just a few months before my big trip to Asia and Europe, during which I circumnavigated the planet. That was also the trip on which I trekked in the Himalayas. Richard was the one person with whom I could have discussions about science, history, philosophy, and other topics at length.

Here, I would like to make a statement about Donald Trump's older brother. As mentioned earlier, Donald Trump had a brother who was eight years older, named Frederick Trump Jr. As a child, Fred Jr. wanted to become a pilot; therefore, he went on to study flying. He became a pilot; however, his authoritarian father lassoed him into his business, which only resulted in Fred Jr.'s demise. Fred Jr. should have just continued with his passion, regardless of the presence or absence of his father. Fred Sr. had "The Plan" for Fred Jr.

In my case, there were some people in my family who had The Plan for me. I am so delighted, as I look back, that I *never* followed their concept of the destiny that I should have. Instead, I paved my own destiny! I decided to *not* allow other people's problems to become my problems, regardless of whether they were inside or outside the family. Because of that, I pursued my own dreams, which involved educating myself, hiking, backpacking, taking road trips, and exotic world travel.

Sometimes, when things go smoothly in life, there are interruptions that occur. I am not talking about minor or smaller things that happen, such as some home repair or an action item in one's life that needs to be addressed. Everyone encounters those types of issues, and, in the end, they do not alter the main trajectory of one's life. The interruptions are when one encounters mischief-makers and troublemakers. These are the types of people who see and know that one has accomplished something in life; however, they are of the envious and mean-spirited type. Here, I am talking about those people who want to build themselves up by tearing others down.

I would like to give an example. A long time ago, I was at a placeholder job, which was a job that I was not intending to stay at for long. We were preparing for a trip to Oklahoma, and I was supposed to meet up with some other people for an assignment. One of the managers presented the following comment to me: "It doesn't take too long to notice that you are knowledgeable about many things. This is a turnoff to many people. When you go on this trip and continue with that, people are *not* going to want to associate with you!"

My response was, basically, to do nothing and say nothing. My thoughts were that such an ignorant statement did not deserve the dignity of a response.

Since I did not change from the time when I was at the university to that position, I thought to myself that I would just continue to be my own true and authentic self. During my many years as an employee at the university, I frequently met people with whom I had discussions about biochemistry, molecular biology, genomics, physics, astronomy, history, and philosophy. My being who I am was *never* a problem then. Why should being the way I am all of a sudden be a problem at that new position?

To answer that, I would like to dissect that manager's foolish statement into its components. The first part—"It doesn't take too long to notice that you are knowledgeable about many things"— indicates that he is aware that I am highly educated; however, *he* is quite troubled by that. Why was nobody troubled by that while I was at the university? When one is working at the university, one encounters many like-minded people who are interested in learning and teaching. The university was an environment that was conducive to learning. I was in my element there!

The second component is: "This is a turnoff to many people." My thoughts simply were that this is *not my* problem! This is *their* problem! This was not the first time that I encountered this type of attitude, and it was not going to be the last time. More on that later. While I was at the university, most people appreciated that I had meaningful information to share with others, which blended into interesting discussions. While I am traveling, I encounter people from various professions, and some of them even are scientists themselves. As one of many examples, I met someone from Europe while I was on a trip to Rapa Nui. When we were at lunch, he overheard some of the other conversations that I had about some of my prior trips and the science that I was involved in. He told me that I came across as a very interesting person. I mentioned, "When I travel, I always meet interesting people, and I enjoy hearing their stories as well." During the lunch and while we were at Anakena beach, we had a deep discussion about ecology, global warming, and other subjects. I was in my element there!

The third component of that statement is: "When you go on this trip and continue with that, people are not going to want to associate with you!" That ended up *not* being exactly true because there were a couple of people whom I was able to have meaningful conversations with. Obviously, that did end up being true with some of those other people; however, my mind remained untroubled by that. When I was in some artificial social situation, such as at a dinner, where people started gossiping or spewing out stupid jokes, I simply remained quiet and uninvolved in that conversation. They are *not* worth my time, and I have *nothing* to contribute to their conversations!

Regarding that manager, I could read into that scheming statement. He was poised to take me down, because it would *not* be possible for me to simply pretend to fit in. I am a person of integrity, and I was on a different wavelength or frequency than he was. He did *feel* it and *sense* it! Then, I felt the sense that he got weirded out by me. I was the polar opposite of him. I sensed that he began to fear me because I acted as a mirror to him. This showed him what he had really become. That made him feel uncomfortable. As they say, "Darkness fears light!"

As time continued, I became keenly aware that this quasi-governmental organization that was funded by the National Science Foundation had many issues. In fact, it was even under congressional investigation for mishandling of financial resources. Many of the people whom I encountered in that organization, as I found out in time, were a bunch of backstabbers, narcissists, hucksters, and even psychopaths. Even though that particular manager resigned and left that organization, there were many other undesirable people who motivated me to leave and seek another and better position, which I did. It all worked out better for me than I expected. Enough said!

This leads to my next observation based upon conversations that I have had with quite a few other people. When I travel overseas, I find it easier to connect with others. In the United States, there is this extreme isolation in which many live in a bubble and are paranoid about other people. I have traveled through Mexico where there is corruption, but it is still culturally rich. I could still interact with people and develop some social relationships with others. I reflect back, and I realize that this was true at the university and in my present position, but it is much more difficult elsewhere in the United States. There is a lot of *consumerism* and *work*, but in reality, those things do *not* really fill the human soul.

As a freethinker, I found people at that placeholder job to be very fake, phony, hyped-up, and often mean-spirited. It was a very cliquish and toxic work environment. This has caused me to realize two things. First, this toxicity has permeated the larger society with different flavors for different regions of the country. Many people are conditioned to be materialistic. The emphasis is upon the external rather than the internal. Simply put, they do not cultivate their inner selves. They have become soulless! They never stop to ask themselves this enlightening question: "What is the point of making a living if all you do every day is work to make a living?" Is this truly living if there's no time to enjoy life? One should demand the freedom to live *and* to think freely! This phrase "making a living" has become nothing but a self-contradiction!

Being a spectator of the artificial social-life situation at that placeholder job, I truly saw how cliques are limiting. This is because cliques are by nature closed and exclusive; therefore, people within them have an attitude and mentality that is very closed and exclusive (or snobby and stuck-up). This means that to fit in, one has to be closed and exclusive themselves. This is exactly why I had a hard time breaking in, because I was *never* on the same wavelength as those people.

It is important to mention that this artificiality and attitude carries over into the political environment at the federal, state, county, and local levels. I have come to see most politicians, including Donald Trump, who is a wannabe politician, to be very fake and phony. As a freethinker, I have made the decision to *not* be affiliated with any political party because I see most of the political factions as glorified cliques. I seek to do what is right, which is to do my civic duty and cast my vote. This involves my becoming informed about the issues and selecting the individual who I believe is the better candidate. Sometimes, this is a choice between the lesser of the evils. Having no political affiliation, I am *not* fettered by any political ideology—or dogma! I seek out the individual who can accomplish more, who will do more good, and who will do less damage.

Donald Trump presented his messages that were expressions of a troubled mind. He used the fear tactic. During his campaign, he was successful at that because many people are conditioned to live in fear and paranoia. He tapped into people's anxiety and state-of-fear consciousness. There have been studies presented that show that the more one watches the news, the more anxious, depressed, and paranoid one can become. Here I would like to interject that one should proceed, while watching the news, with the intention to be informed and empowered. It is understandable that this is not easy because of all the sensationalism, advertisements, and content that are not really newsworthy. Most media outlets want to keep people's minds troubled or in some state of anxiety.

Being a practitioner of meditation, I observe my train of thought, and I have become aware of the subtle psychological influences television programming has. Television programming does want to program minds, because, behind it, there are products to be sold as well as business to be made. As a freethinker, I seek to prevent my mind from being cluttered with sensationalism, hype, fear, and junk! I simply distill out the facts (events as they transpire in time) from the rest of the noise. Knowledge of things should empower people—not scare them. With that knowledge, one can allow oneself to take steps to prevent issues from arising and to make the right decisions. Obviously, with some things, surprises can occur. For example, one does not know in advance exactly when a tornado will strike or an earthquake will happen. When it comes to a hurricane, though, there are steps that can be taken to prepare.

There is legitimate fear. When there is real danger involved, it is normal and necessary for survival; however, many people in the US are psychologically living in a mode of fear about everything. It may even be to the point that it is pathological, as it dominates their state of mind and consciousness. It becomes excessive, and they even start to fear things that don't exist.

Getting back on track, it is important to know what is happening in the various locations around the world. I want to know what is happening in Yemen, Nigeria, Ghana, China, Russia, and anywhere else on the planet. Whatever political discourse is occurring, war is being fought, or natural disaster is happening does have a bearing on our lives. Being a free and informed thinker, I can understand things in their larger historical contexts and observe the directions things are going. Being educated in science and history, I can then interpret what transpires through that prism. After all, history is constantly being made.

In addition to being interested in science and history, I was very interested in philosophy in college. I even minored in philosophy while I majored in biochemistry. I was particularly interested in ancient Greek and Roman philosophy and Eastern philosophies. I enjoyed Pythagoras, Socrates, Plato, Aristotle, Heraclitus, Zeno, Cleanthes, Chrysippus, Marcus Cicero, and Marcus Aurelius. I was also interested in the history of science and the philosophy of science.

To make a long story short, I started my life in the Roman Catholic and Lutheran churches. I had a falling out with one of the Lutheran groups; therefore, I made the decision to sever myself from Christianity completely. For a while, I followed many of the principles of the Roman Stoic philosophers. Concurrently, I studied the philosophies of Buddhism, Taoism, and Confucianism. Having read the Bible in German and in English from cover to cover, I formulated my own opinions on what I could accept and reject. I studied some of the other religions also, such as Islam, Judaism, Zoroastrianism, and Sikhism. I was interested in the history of those religions and their teachings. I even spent some time reading portions of their sacred writings.

My reasons for going on my own path by escaping religion were the fakeness and pretentiousness of going through the motions with others in groups. I was exposed to two or more sets of religious dogmas, and I found deep down that those teachings contradicted what I experienced in my life. My experiences were real; therefore, the ecclesiastical doctrines had no value for me. By moving on, I discovered an authentic life—inner and outer. I preferred it to the confinement of dogmatic shackles and any religious or political parties. I became liberated and saw life more clearly. I also saw a bigger picture, *and* I wanted to see more, which was another reason why I proceeded with my world travels. It often feels better to me to be alone than to compromise my truth and to conform to the fakery of others! I prefer the solace of the wilderness and inner authenticity. It is far more valuable and true than the hassle of dealing with others and the pretentiousness and lies that go along with it. Marcus Aurelius, who was a Stoic philosopher and Roman emperor, stated, "The object in life is not to be on the side of the majority, but to escape finding oneself in the ranks of the insane." Also, I noticed that devotees to some churches hand out simple answers about people who leave. They believe that we leave the church to pursue hedonism. No! We leave to search for the truth outside the framework of any organized religion.

I approached all those subjects because I have an intellectual curiosity. Being unaffiliated with any particular religion, I felt that I was a freethinker there as well. Just like everything else, I accept what makes sense to me, and I reject what I don't like. The result is that I have my own philosophy of life that is uniquely my own. There have been many things that I have learned in the classroom; however, there are many things that I determine on my own.

I learn many things directly from books. Much of what I have learned has been through my world travels. Many things are learned through meaningful conversations with people. There are times when I speak. There are times when I listen. There are times when I need to teach. There are times when I need to keep silent and learn. It is important to broaden one's understanding, yet I try to have an in-depth understanding of many subjects as well. Regardless of how well I know a subject, there is always more to be learned.

Over the years and even decades, there are many who see that I have morphed into someone who is completely different from the person they originally knew. There are those who are very accepting and are happy that I am a much happier person. They realize that I am unfettered by so much junk that many people are attached to. There are others who want to push back; however, I could care less. That is fine with me because that presents a filter to those who were and are truly my friends. False friends are *gone*! Hooray! I believe that some people are in one's life for a reason. Others are there just for a season.

Importantly, people should have freedom *from* religion if they want to, as it is in my case. Oh! Regarding the fundamentalist evangelical Christians, Jehovah's Witnesses, and Mormons who come knocking on my door, I am not obligated to open my door to anyone I do not recognize. I only open my door to friends, family, and service personnel whom I have hired.

Of course, New Age and pop psychology thinking has also encroached into the society. An example of pop psychology is a book that was written by Norman Vincent Peale, *The Power of Positive Thinking*, which was published in 1952. Peale developed a fascination with psychiatry as an answer that nearly all basic problems are personal for his congregation at the Marble Collegiate Church in New York City.[1] He believed that we live in a world that is mental more than physical. In fact, Norman Vincent Peale was one of the three major people who influenced Donald Trump's life. (The other two were his father and Roy Cohn.) Trump is a Norman Vincent Peale disciple.

What is wrong is that Peale believed that thoughts and attitudes literally control and shape the physical properties of time and space around and in a person's life. It is common sense that thoughts and attitudes influence reality; however, thoughts are *not* the building blocks of the universe in the manner that subatomic particles are.

These people see the world through rose-colored glasses. They frequently are in denial of reality (and will deny other people's realities also, if they don't fit in with theirs) and anything that doesn't fit into the world they choose. Sorry, but the laws of physics cannot be violated. They don't bend to suit Peale's followers' reality. One of these days, I will challenge these believers to create their own reality in which they can walk through solid walls and jump off buildings and fly. Let's see if any of them rise to the task.

The bottom line for many New Agers is that they make claims that they are spiritual; however, they are not truth seekers. They wish to create their own truth but deny any truth out there that doesn't fit into their world. Reality is far more complicated than that, as is evident to me by studying science.

Although thoughts cannot control the properties of space and time, they can have great influence. Thought does have tremendous power. The mind is intricately connected to the body. The mind acts upon the body, and the body reacts upon the mind. Usually, a healthy mind means a healthy body. When the mind is agitated, then the body also becomes disturbed. There are such things known as psychosomatic illnesses, which is one of the subjects in psychiatry. Stress adversely affects the mind and body.

Also, if the thoughts are well-grounded, they can become clear, continuous, and deep. It is unfortunate that many people do not know what deep thinking is with so much confusion in their minds most of the time. After the interview that I had with the Tibetan Buddhist lama, I began practicing meditation daily. That was about thirty years ago. I have learned how to discipline the mind, and I have become more grounded. Meanwhile, I am aware that I have a lot more work to do. I am working on silencing my thoughts. Through my practice, I aspire to have my thoughts and mental images become clearer, stronger, more focused, and well defined instead of distorted. Thoughts are the sources of actions.

If the thoughts are focused, then the resultant actions have greater impact. One of my meditation techniques involves watching my thoughts with vigilance and action. If evil thoughts are rooted out, then the actions performed will not be evil.

I have learned that, if I have control over my thoughts and have a focused mind, I am able to be productive in my life and produce immense work. As examples, my world trips started as thoughts, which then went into the planning stages. These stages involved purchasing my airline tickets, preparing and collecting my documents, packing, and any other relevant preparations. Being the seasoned traveler that I am, I travel lightly. In the same way I try to keep my mind uncluttered, I keep my travel packing uncluttered. The bottom line is that, if one puts one's mind to something, it can be achieved—of course, with limitations. After all, the laws of physics can't be violated. I can't fly through the air. I need an airplane or some other transportation to get me to my destination.

Returning to the topic about free and independent thinkers, I do not naturally conform to any group or establishment. I have friends, however, who are living in different places. Some live in the same town as I do, and others are elsewhere in the United States and other countries. Often, I associate in small groups of like-minded people with similar interests or views. Because people in those groups come and go, those associations are usually temporary. At the same time, I have no attachment or identity to any group. I have an inner circle of friends, but I tend to freely move between groups and acquaintances, depending upon circumstances and time. Since I am not a conformist, I do not follow any political party or organized religion. And as I mentioned earlier, I do not like being in crowds.

Having no identity with any groups or organizations of any kind, I prefer to be an independent thinker. An exception is that I am a member of a professional organization, the Institute of

Electrical and Electronics Engineers (IEEE); it serves as a vehicle for technical, scientific, and engineering information. After all, I want to remain informed about the recent advances in technology, computer science, and cybersecurity.

As I mentioned above, being a freethinker, I pursued my own dreams. I encountered those individuals who build themselves up by tearing others down, such as that manager, who was basically an ignorant fool! I have also encountered the naysayers. These are people who made excuses for me regarding why I shouldn't take part in an endeavor. I am so glad, looking back, that I just had a strong will and ignored their advice completely. Those were foolish people who had given up on their dreams. Because I *never* allowed them to convince me to give up on my aspirations and endeavors, I was able to be successful at many things. These included trekking in the Himalayas; climbing Mount Kilimanjaro, Mount Kinabalu, Popocatépetl, Volcán Pacaya, and Volcán Villarrica; trekking in the Andes; backpacking in the Grand Canyon in Arizona sixteen times; and the list goes on.

Just like the wolf, I do *not* concern myself with the opinions of sheep!

CONCLUSIONS

*"Questions of ecology can't be separated from economics. . . .
[E]nvironmental destruction isn't caused by ignorance or mistaken
policies: it is the inevitable result of a social and economic system
that puts profit before people and must constantly expand to survive.
There can be no permanent solution to the environmental crisis
so long as capitalism continues."*
—Ian Angus, editor of *Climate & Capitalism* (2011)

This is a book about Donald Trump. At the same time, it is not just about Donald Trump because I also describe political situations in the United States and elsewhere in the world. In addition, I have included descriptions of my various travels around the world and the insights that I obtained from those trips. This presents a perspective outside the political arena. It also means that the problems, though real and difficult, can be dealt with.

There is a great deal of turmoil in Washington, DC. Also, there is a lot of vitriol and acrimony. What is true is that many of those political and environmental problems will be around for a while; however, there are potential solutions. I describe my trips alongside the problems of the world. Meanwhile, many officials elected by the people who are in Washington have not truly experienced much of what the world has to offer.

As of this writing, Donald Trump has been deeply embroiled in the tumult of investigations, court hearings, and lawsuits, and I wonder about his ability to govern. It seems that most of his domestic and foreign policies in the past were conducted on Twitter. Of course, there have been times when he has presented himself as a showpiece for public consumption, such as when he signed an executive order or a bill that passed the US Congress. Yes, this circus atmosphere makes me wonder!

When I observe Donald Trump, he comes across as an egomaniac. Many things that come forth from his mouth are just plain ridiculous. Even though he is a political outsider, he has certainly learned the ropes of the Washington insiders. In many ways, just like Vladimir Putin, he has become an authoritarian oligarch. It seems that the oligarchical nature of both Bush administrations has transferred to the Trump administration.

People often speak about Trump's wealth. He has been in his real-estate and casino businesses for a long time. Then, I ask myself, how significant is his wealth? He has been involved with many lawsuits. He has been embroiled in investigations of people around him. Many of the people around him also have oligarchical tendencies. In time, the dark truths will be made manifest. Just like the iceberg, 90 percent of it is under the water. Who knows what is lurking beneath the political surface.

Who genuinely wants to be in Trump's position? I know that I would not want to be embroiled in his lawsuits. I would not want to have his health problems. He is consumed with the three poisons of greed, anger, and ignorance. Having monetary wealth, he was greedy and possessed a craving for power. He obtained that power as president of the United States. Let us not forget that it is as easy to lose that power as it is to obtain. Conquest is easy, but control isn't! Trump is a very angry person. This is because he has a very thin skin. It is apparent in how offended he becomes and how he reacts to other people's comments on X in a very bellicose manner! Many of his constituents are angry people like him, and, like birds of a feather, they flock together. The Trump rallies are very expressive of the emotion of anger. It is evident, as Donald Trump presents angry speeches among angry constituents. And having been involved with various investigations makes him an even angrier person.

Donald Trump is not an unintelligent person, but he expresses ignorance and stupidity. Bragging that he does not read books signifies that he chooses to remain ignorant about many subject matters. Meanwhile, there is another kind of ignorance that involves how aware he is of his own actions. Having been in the position of president, Trump had to be flexible at times; however, when a particular position or stance of his changed depending upon who was in the room with him or whom he had a meeting with, it made me wonder whether he remembered what he said when speaking with different people. He is also ignorant of the common person, as he has not lived in any impoverished situation. He was brought up in a well-to-do family; therefore, he did not have to struggle the way many students have to struggle, balancing academic work and holding a job at the same time. In this regard, he had it easy! He may interface with the common people at campaign rallies, but these are public-relations activities to get people worked up so that they will vote for him.

As I look back at my life, I am glad that I did not get into any lawsuits. I have always had the philosophy that avoiding lawyers is good. The need for the services of a lawyer has been almost non-existent for me, with the exception of some small clerical matters.

I have been prudent in my financial affairs, such that I have saved for my trips. Importantly, I am happy that I decided to travel to those places around the world where I have gone. Just as important, I have very good health, fitness, and stamina, which allow me to engage in endeavors such as hiking, backpacking, and mountain climbing. I intend to continue those activities and travel to more places around the world.

One final note needs to be added, which is that since I started this book, the coronavirus pandemic has happened worldwide.

The new challenges presented can be summarized by Daniel Yergin as follows:

> When it comes to transportation, people may revert to preferring to "own" their mobility—their personal car—rather than buying mobility when they need it, and, at least for a few years, opt to drive rather than fly when there is a choice. They will also be more cautious about using public transportation. The trend toward digitalization, broadly-defined—new ways of working enabled by digital technologies, trading the physical world for the virtual world—has suddenly moved into hyper-gear. Work need not be concentrated in offices, companies can be run from homes, newspapers can be put out with almost no one in the newsroom; time spent commuting can be reduced; business meetings can be replaced by digital connecting. These impacts will last after lockdowns are well in the past. It took three years after 9/11 and more than seven years after the 2008 financial crisis for air travel in the United States to recover to the previous levels. The acceleration of innovation, especially in terms of artificial intelligence and machine learning and automation, will bring change for all kinds of work.[1]

This pandemic has, back in 2020 and 2021, caused me to postpone certain international travel plans for a while; however, my road tips have continued. Fortunately, with the waning of the pandemic, my international trips have started up again. This is how I was able to get to Ecuador in 2022, including the Galapagos, to Chihuahua and Sinaloa in Mexico, and, more recently, to Peru, Bolivia, and Japan.

It is through my travel experiences that I have enriched my life. In addition, I have come to understand how the natural world works, how the human world works, and how nature and humans interact. I have come to understand many of the world's problems, whether they are ecological, political, social, or cultural. When one travels to local and distant parts of the world, it is always an educational experience. Even though I have an extensive education, including graduate school, education outside the classroom has never ceased for me. Reading books on a large variety of subjects is educational. Watching scientific and historical programs on PBS is educational.

Regarding the major point of being wealthier than Donald Trump, I would like to affirm that true wealth is not only contingent upon how much money one has in the bank. People can have a wealth of experience. There are many that consider their health a source of wealth. In my case, it is my good health and travel experience, which is a continuation of my education, that contributes to my wealth. I have experienced the accomplishments of climbing many mountain summits; exploring many tropical rainforests, deserts, and temperate regions; interfacing with many cultures around the world; and treating those as opportunities to enrich my life. That list can go on. My experiences in the Amazon, Tibet, the Himalayas, the Grand Canyon in Arizona, and the Kalahari in Namibia can't be taken away from me. My experiences of learning about the local cultures, the flora, and the fauna has caused me to become even more intellectually curious. This also means learning about the local issues of the places that I have visited.

Trump may be wealthy financially; however, does he have peace in his life? With all of the lawsuits, criminal indictments, and trials that he is embroiled in, when will he have peace and happiness in his life? With all of his hate, anger, and vitriol that he expresses, is this the sign of an untroubled mind? Definitely not! Here, I will suggest that a component of true wealth can be the absence of something. I am referring to the absence of legal issues, criminal cases, and all of the other drama. I consider myself wealthy by having the absence of such troubles and hyper-excitement in my life. Most of the time, my life is very peaceful, affording the opportunity to meditate and have access to Nature to provide me with peace of mind. Good health, peace, sound intellect, and experience with my world travels is MY TRUE WEALTH!

ENDNOTES

Chapter 1

[1] Donald Trump: President of United States, https://www.britannica.com/biography/Donald-Trump.

[2] "Trump's parents and siblings: What do we know of them?" *BBC News,* October 3, 2018, https://www.bbc.com/news/world-us-canada-45731931.

[3] Jason Horowitz, "Donald Trump's Old Queens Neighborhood Contrasts with the Diverse Area Around It," *The New York Times,* September 22, 2015, https://www.nytimes.com/2015/09/23/us/politics/donald-trumps-old-queens-neighborhood-now-a-melting-pot-was-seen-as-a-cloister.html).

[4] Jack Jenkins and Maina Mwaura, "Exclusive: Trump, confirmed a Presbyterian, now identifies as 'non-denominational Christian,'" *Religion News Service,* October 23, 2020, https://web.archive.org/web/20201024120658/https://religionnews.com/2020/10/23/exclusive-trump-confirmed-a-presbyterian-now-identifies-as-non-denominational-christian/.

[5] Michael Kranish and Marc Fisher, *Revealed: The Definitive Biography of the 45th President* (New York: Scribner, 2017), 38, https://books.google.com/books?id=x2jUDQAAQBAJ&pg=PA38.

[6] "Two Hundred and Twelfth Commencement for the Conferring of Degrees," University of Pennsylvania (May 20, 1968): 19–21, https://web.archive.org/web/20160719213709/https://www.archives.upenn.edu/primdocs/upg/upg7/upg7_1968.pdf. Archived from the original, https://www.archives.upenn.edu/primdocs/upg/upg7/upg7_1968.pdf, on July 19, 2016.

[7] Frank Rich, "The Original Donald Trump," *New York Magazine* (April 30, 2018): https://nymag.com/daily/intelligencer/2018/04/frank-rich-roy-cohn-the-original-donald-trump.html.

[8] "Trump Organization Inc/The," Bloomberg, https://www.bloomberg.com/profile/company/3603126Z:US.

[9] William E. Geist, "The Expanding Empire of Donald Trump," *The New York Times* (April 8, 1984): https://www.nytimes.com/1984/04/08/magazine/the-expanding-empire-of-donald-trump.html; Sara Wooten, *Donald Trump: From Real Estate to Reality TV* (Berkeley Heights, NJ: Enslow Publishers, Inc., 2009), 32–35.

[10] Gwenda Blair, *The Trumps: Three Generations of Builders and a President* (New York: Simon & Schuster, 2001), 300.

[11] Alessandra Stanley, "The Other Trump," *The New York Times* (October 1, 2016): https://www.nytimes.com/2016/10/02/fashion/tiffany-the-other-trump.html.

[12] Michael Shnayerson, "Inside Ivana's Role in Donald Trump's Empire," *Vanity Fair* (January 2, 1988).

[13] Associated Press, "Ivana Trump to write memoir about raising US president's children," *The Guardian* (March 16, 2017): https://www.theguardian.com/us-news/2017/mar/16/ivana-trump-write-memoir-about-raising-us-presidents-donald-children.

[14] William E. Geist, "The Expanding Empire of Donald Trump," *The New York Times* (April 8, 1984): https://www.nytimes.com/1984/04/08/magazine/the-expanding-empire-of-donald-trump.html.

[15] Dan McQuade, "The Truth About the Rise and Fall of Donald Trump's Atlantic City Empire," *Philadelphia* (August 16, 2015). Retrieved March 21, 2016.

[16] Wolfgang Saxon, "Trump Buys Hilton's Hotel in Atlantic City," *The New York Times*. (Retrieved May 25, 2023).

[17] Lenny Glynn (April 8, 1990). "Trump's Taj—Open at Last, With a Scary Appetite," *The New York Times*.

[18] Jonathan Greenberg, "Trump lied to me about his wealth to get onto the Forbes 400. Here are the tapes," *The Washington Post* (April 20, 2018).

[19] Steven Wishnia, "How Rent-Stabilized Tenants Foiled Donald Trump," Metropolitan Council on Housing (April 2016): *METCouncilOnHousing.org*.

[20] Charles V Bagli, "Trump Group Selling West Side Parcel for $1.8 billion," *The New York Times* (May 17, 2016): https://www.nytimes.com/2005/06/01/nyregion/trump-group-selling-west-side-parcel-for-18-billion.html.

[21] "Trump's Plaza Hotel Bankruptcy Plan Approved," *The New York Times*, Reuters (December 12, 1992): https://www.nytimes.com/1992/12/12/business/company-news-trump-s-plaza-hotel-bankruptcy-plan-approved.html.

[22] Clare O'Connor, "Fourth Time's a Charm: How Donald Trump Made Bankruptcy Work for Him," *Forbes* (April 29, 2011): https://www.forbes.com/sites/clareoconnor/2011/04/29/fourth-times-a-charm-how-donald-trump-made-bankruptcy-work-for-him/).

[23] Emily Flitter, "Art of the spin: Trump bankers question his portrayal of financial comeback," Reuters: https://www.reuters.com/article/us-usa-election-trump-bankruptcies-insig/art-of-the-spin-trump-bankers-question-his-portrayal-of-financial-comeback-idUSKCN0ZX0GP.

[24] Chase Peterson-Withorn, "Donald Trump Has Gained More Than $100 Million on Mar-a-Lago," *Forbes* (April 23, 2018): https://www.forbes.com/sites/chasewithorn/2018/04/23/donald-trump-has-gained-more-than-100-million-on-mar-a-lago/; John Koblin, "Trump Sells Miss Universe Organization to WME-IMG Talent Agency," *The New York Times* (September 14, 2015): https://www.nytimes.com/2015/09/15/business/media/trump-sells-miss-universe-organization-to-wme-img-talent-agency.html.

[25] Zach Love, "Bankruptcy Roundup: Trump Dumps Casinos, Fortunoff Gets Sued, and Peanut Corp. Goes Under," *Law.Com* (Feb. 17, 2009); John Koblin, "Trump Sells Miss Universe Organization to WME-IMG Talent Agency," *The New York Times* (September 14, 2015): https://www.nytimes.com/2015/09/15/business/media/trump-sells-miss-universe-organization-to-wme-img-talent-agency.html.

[26] Andrew Buncombe, "Trump boasted about writing many books—his ghostwriter says otherwise," *The Independent* (July 4, 2018): https://www.independent.co.uk/news/world/americas/us-politic s/trump-books-tweet-ghostwriter-tim-o-brien-tony-schwartz-writer-response-a8431271.html.

[27] Jane Mayer, "Donald Trump's Ghostwriter Tells All," *The New Yorker* (July 18, 2016): https://www.newyorker.com/magazine/2016/07/25/donald-trumps-ghostwriter-tells-all.

[28] Seth Gitell, "I Survived Trump University," *Politico* (March 8,

2016): https://www.politico.com/magazine/story/2016/03/i-sur-vived-trump-university-213710; William D. Cohan, "Big Hair on Campus: Did Donald Trump Defraud Thousands of Real Estate Students?" *Vanity Fair* (December 3, 2013): https://www.vanityfair.com/news/2014/01/trump-university-fraud-scandal.

[29] Samuel Maull, "Trump, Maples Officially Divorced," Associated Press (June 9, 1999): https://apnews.com/article/145e1dc-c5633e34b3f45485004e9dcec.

[30] Mary L. Trump, *Too Much and Never Enough,* New York: Simon & Schuster (2020): 135–36.

[31] Richard Winger, "Donald Trump Ran for President in 2000 in Several Reform Party Presidential Primaries," *Ballot Access News* (2011): https://ballot-access.org/2011/12/25/donald-trump-ranfor-president-in-2000-in-several-reform-party-presidential-primaries/; Adam Nagourney, "Reform Bid Said to Be a No-Go for Trump," *The New York Times* (February 14, 2000): https://archive.nytimes.com/www.nytimes.com/library/politics/camp/021400wh-ref-trump.html.

[32] Michael M. Grynbaum and Ashley Parker, "Donald Trump the Political Showman, Born on 'The Apprentice,'" The New York Times (July 16, 2016): https://www.nytimes.com/2016/07/17/business/media/donald-trump-apprentice.html.

[33] Cynthia Littleton, "Donald Trump to Remain Executive Producer on 'Celebrity Apprentice,'" *Variety* (December 8, 2016).

[34] Ewen MacAskill, "Donald Trump bows out of 2012 US presidential election race," *The Guardian* (May 16, 2011): https://www.theguardian.com/world/2011/may/16/donald-trump-us-presidential-race.

[35] Adam B. Lerner, "The 10 best lines from Donald Trump's announcement speech," *Politico* (June 16, 2015): https://www.politico.com/story/2015/06/donald-trump-2016-announcement-10-best-lines-119066.

[36] Elspeth Reeve, "How Donald Trump Evolved From a Joke to an Almost Serious Candidate," *The New Republic* (October 27, 2015): https://newrepublic.com/article/123228/how-donald-trump-evolved-joke-almost-serious-candidate.

[37] Noah Bierman, "Donald Trump helps bring far-right media's edgier elements into the mainstream," Los Angeles Times (August 22, 2016): https://www.latimes.com/politics/la-na-pol-trump-media-20160820-

snap-story.html; German Lopez, "We need to stop acting like Trump isn't pandering to white supremacists," *Vox* (August 14, 2017): https://www.vox.com/policy-and-politics/2017/8/13/16140504/trump-charlottesville-white-supremacists.

[38] Matthew Nussbaum, "RNC Chairman: Trump is our nominee," *Politico* (May 3, 2016): https://www.politico.com/blogs/2016-gop-primary-live-updates-and-results/2016/05/reince-priebus-donald-trump-is-nominee-222767; Ivan Levingston, "Donald Trump officially names Mike Pence for VP," CNBC (July 15, 2016): https://www.cnbc.com/2016/07/15/donald-trump-officially-names-mike-pence-as-his-vp.html; "Trump closes the deal, becomes Republican nominee for president," *Fox News* (July 15, 2016): https://www.foxnews.com/politics/2016/07/19/republicans-start-process-to-nominate-trump-for-president.html.

[39] Carol D. Leonnig, Rosalind S. Helderman, and Anne Gearan, "Clinton e-mail review could find security issues," *The Washington Post* (March 6, 2015); Ken Dilanian, "Clinton Emails Held Indirect References to Undercover CIA Officers," *NBC News* (February 4, 2016).

[40] Alan Rappeport, "Donald Trump Breaks with Recent History by Not Releasing Tax Returns," *The New York Times* (May 11, 2016): https://www.nytimes.com/politics/first-draft/2016/05/11/donald-trump-breaks-with-recent-history-by-not-releasing-tax-returns/; Chris Isidore and Jeanne Sahadi, "Trump says he can't release tax returns because of audits," CNN (February 26, 2016): https://money.cnn.com/2016/02/26/pf/taxes/trump-tax-returns-audit/.

[41] Shane Goldmacher and Ben Schreckinger, "Trump pulls off biggest upset in U.S. history," *Politico* (November 9, 2016): https://www.politico.com/story/2016/11/election-results-2016-clinton-trump-231070; Drew Desilver, "Trump's victory another example of how Electoral College wins are bigger than popular vote ones," Pew Research Center (December 20, 2016): https://www.pewresearch.org/fact-tank/2016/12/20/why-electoral-college-landslides-are-easier-to-win-than-popular-vote-ones/.

[42] Nate Cohn, "Why Trump Won: Working-Class Whites," *The New York Times* (November 9, 2016): https://www.nytimes.com/2016/11/10/upshot/why-trump-won-working-class-whites.html.

[43] Tina Brown, "Donald Trump, Settling Down," *The Washington Post* (January 27, 2005): retrieved May 7, 2017.

[44] Michael S. Schmidt, Eric Lipton, and Charlie Savage, "Jared Kushner, Trump's Son-in-Law, Is Cleared to Serve as Adviser," *The New York Times* (January 21, 2017): https://www.nytimes.com/2017/01/21/us/politics/donald-trump-jared-kushner-justice-department.html; "Ivanka Trump's new job," VVB, *The Economist* (March 31, 2017): https://www.economist.com/blogs/democracyinamerica/2017/03/family-affair.

[45] David E. Sanger, "Putin Ordered 'Influence Campaign' Aimed at U.S. Election, Report Says," *The New York Times* (January 6, 2017): https://www.nytimes.com/2017/01/06/us/politics/russia-hack-report.html.

[46] Jeff Nesbit, "Donald Trump's Many, Many, Many, Many Ties to Russia," *Time* (August 2, 2016): https://time.com/4433880/donald-trump-ties-to-russia/.

[47] Ned Parker, Jonathan Landay, and Warren Strobel, "Exclusive: Trump campaign had at least 18 undisclosed contacts with Russians: sources," Reuters (May 18, 2017): https://www.reuters.com/article/us-usa-trump-russia-contacts-idUSKCN18E106.

[48] David A. Graham, "We Still Don't Know What Happened Between Trump and Russia," *The Atlantic* (November 15, 2019): https://www.theatlantic.com/ideas/archive/2019/11/we-still-dont-know-what-happened-between-trump-and-russia/602116/.

[49] Philip Bump, "Analysis | Trump and the White House have denied Russian collusion more than 140 times," *The Washington Post* (January 11, 2018): https://www.washingtonpost.com/news/politics/wp/2018/01/11/trump-and-the-white-house-have-denied-russian-collusion-more-than-140-times/.

[50] Mary L. Trump, *Too Much and Never Enough*, New York: Simon & Schuster (2020): 15–16.

[51] ———, 44.

[52] Heidi M. Przybyla and Fredreka Schouten, "At 2.6 million strong, Women's Marches crush expectations," *USA Today* (January 21, 2017): https://www.usatoday.com/story/news/politics/2017/01/21/womens-march-aims-start-movement-trump-inauguration/96864158/.

[53] David Smith, "Trump's billionaire cabinet could be the wealthiest administration ever," *The Guardian* (December 2, 2016); Susan Page, "Analysis: Trump's Cabinet dubbed 'Goldman, generals and gazillionaires,'" *USA Today* (December 11, 2016); Matthew Cooper, "Donald Trump Is Building the Most Conservative Presidential Cabinet In U.S. History," *Newsweek* (December 9, 2016).

[54] Michael S. Schmidt, Eric Lipton, and Charlie Savage, "Jared Kushner, Trump's Son-in-Law, Is Cleared to Serve as Adviser," *The New York Times* (January 21, 2017): https://www.nytimes.com/2017/01/21/us/politics/donald-trump-jared-kushner-justice-department.html.

[55] Aidan Quigley, "All of Trump's executive actions so far," *Politico* (January 25, 2017): https://www.politico.com/agenda/story/2017/01/all-trump-executive-actions-000288.

[56] Brady Dennis, "As Syria embraces Paris climate deal, it's the United States against the world," *The Washington Post* (November 7, 2017).

[57] Jacob Pramuk and Christina Wilkie, "Trump declares national emergency to build border wall, setting up massive legal fight," CNBC (February 15, 2019).

[58] Thomas Carothers and Frances Z. Brown, "Can U.S. Democracy Policy Survive Trump?" Carnegie Endowment for International Peace (October 1, 2018).

[59] Megan Carpentier, "Trump's supreme court picks: from Tea Party senator to anti-abortion crusader," *The Guardian* (September 24, 2016).

[60] Josh Gerstein, "A closer look at Trump's potential Supreme Court nominees," *Politico* (January 3, 2017).

[61] Ashley Killough, "GOP triggers nuclear option on Neil Gorsuch nomination," *CNN Politics* (Archived from the original on April 11, 2019).

[62] Mark Landle and Maggie Haberman, "Brett Kavanaugh Is Trump's Pick for Supreme Court," *The New York Times* (July 9, 2018): archived from the original on July 10, 2018.

[63] Jacob Pramuk and Christina Wilkie, "Trump declares national emergency to build border wall, setting up massive legal fight," CNBC (February 15, 2019); William Cummings, "'A WALL is a WALL!' Trump declares. But his definition has shifted a lot over time," *USA*

Today (January 8, 2019): archived from the original on July 25, 2019.

[64] Lolita Baldor, "Congress warns Pentagon not to move money to fund Trump wall," Associated Press (February 26, 2020): archived from the original on June 3, 2020.

[65] Chloe Farand, "Donald Trump Disassembles 90 Federal State Regulations in Just Over a Month in White House," *The Independent* (March 6, 2017): archived from the original on March 8, 2021.

[66] Nadja Popovich, Livia Albeck-Ripka, and Kendra Pierre-Louis, "The Trump Administration Rolled Back More Than 100 Environmental Rules. Here's the Full List," *The New York Times* (January 20, 2021).

[67] Michael Greshko, Laura Parker, Brian Clark Howard, Daniel Stone, Alejandra Borunda, and Sarah Gibbens, "Trump proposes cuts to climate and clean-energy programs," National Geographic Society (February 12, 2018).

[68] "Trump to sign new order rolling back Obama energy regs," *Fox News* (March 28, 2017): archived from the original on April 16, 2017.

[69] Aamer Madhani and Jill Colvin, "A farewell to @realDonaldTrump, gone after 57,000 tweets," Associated Press (January 9, 2021).

[70] Elizabeth Landers, "Spicer: Tweets are Trump's official statements," CNN (June 6, 2017): archived from the original on July 20, 2017.

[71] Mary L. Trump, *Too Much and Never Enough*. New York: Simon & Schuster (2020): p 199.

[72] A Complete Guide to All 17 (Known) Trump and Russia Investigations, https://www.wired.com/story/mueller-investigation-trump-russia-complete-guide/.

[73] Mary L. Trump, *Too Much and Never Enough*, New York: Simon & Schuster (2020): 140.

[74] ——— 197–98.

[75] ——— 197–98.

[76] Michael D'Antonio, "The psychologist in the Trump family speaks," CNN (June 17, 2020).

[77] Mary L. Trump, *Too Much and Never Enough*, New York: Simon & Schuster, 202.

[78] ——— 202.

[79] ——— 204–5.

[80] —— 207–8.
[81] —— 207–8.

Chapter 2

[1] David Nakamura, Dana Hedgpeth, and Sari Horwitz, "Videos show details of Tucson shooting," *The Washington Post* (January 19, 2011).

[2] Amanda Terkel, "Clarence Dupnik, Arizona Sheriff, Criticized by Sen. Jon Kyl Over Shooting Comments (VIDEO)" *Huffington Post* (May 25, 2011).

[3] "Love Canal–Public Health Time Bomb," Archived from the original on February 2, 2017: http://health.ny.gov.

[4] Dennis B. Roddy and Vivian Nereim (April 6, 2010), "A history of violations at Upper Big Branch Mine," Pittsburgh Post-Gazette.

Chapter 3

[1] John Powers, *Introduction to Tibetan Buddhism* (Rev. ed.), Ithaca, New York: Snow Lion Publications, 392–3, 415.

[2] J. Takakusu, trans, *The Life of Vasubandhu by Paramartha*, T'oung-pao 5 (1904): 269–96.

[3] Jay L. Garfield, *The Fundamental Wisdom of the Middle Way*, Oxford: Oxford University Press (1995).

[4] Tsepon W. D. Shakabpa, *Tibet: A Political History*, New Haven and London: Yale University Press (1967): 25.

[5] John Powers, *Introduction to Tibetan Buddhism*, Snow Lion Publications (2007): 467.

[6] The Gelug School of Tibetan Buddhism, https://www.learnreligions. com/the-gelug-school-of-tibetan-buddhism-449627.

[7] Efraín Ríos Montt, https://en.wikipedia.org/wiki/Efra%C3%ADn_R%C3%ADos_Montt.

Chapter 4

[1] Jared Diamond, *Collapse: How Societies Choose to Fail or Succeed*, Penguin Books (2005): 79–119.

[2] *Easter Island—Where Giants Walked,* https://www.youtube.com/watch?v=7j08gxUcBgc.

[3] Gymnosperm Database, *Fitzroya cupressoides*.

[4] C. Vézina, A. Kudelski, and SN Sehgal, "Rapamycin (AY-22,989), a

new antifungal antibiotic. I. Taxonomy of the producing streptomycete and isolation of the active principle," *The Journal of Antibiotics* (October 1975): 28 (10), 721–6.

[5] R. van Der Heijden et al, "The catharanthus alkaloids: pharmacognosy and biotechnology," *Current Medicinal Chemistry* (2004): 11 (5): 607–28. doi:10.2174/0929867043455846. PMID 15032608.

[6] Royal Botanic Gardens Kew, https://powo.science.kew.org/taxon/urn:lsid:ipni.org:names:147776-1.

[7] Tree SA, https://treesa.org/erythrina-abyssinica.

[8] Royal Botanic Gardens Kew, https://powo.science.kew.org/taxon/urn:lsid:ipni.org:names:81519-1.

[9] PlantZAfrica, *Ochna pulchra*, https://pza.sanbi.org/ochna-pulchra.

[10] A. W. Gentry and W. Morawetz, "Bignoniaceae: Part II (Tribe Tecomeae)," *Flora Neotropica* (1992): 25 (2): 51–104. JSTOR 4393739.

[11] The Plant List, *Bignoniaceae,* http://www.theplantlist.org/browse/A/Bignoniaceae).

[12] JSTOR Global Plants, *Lonchocarpus capassa*, https://plants.jstor.org/compilation/lonchocarpus.capassa.

[13] The Plant List, "*Adansonia digitata* L.," Retrieved 21 November 2015.

[14] "Entry for *Sclerocarya birrea*," JSTOR Global Plants, JSTOR.

[15] PlantZAfrica, *Ansellia Africana*, http://pza.sanbi.org/ansellia-africana.

[16] The Plant List, *Nyctaginaceae,* http://www.theplantlist.org/browse/A/Nyctaginaceae.

[17] Bruyns Endress ME, "A revised classification of the Apocynaceae s.l.," (PDF), *The Botanical Review* PV (2000): 66 (1): 1–56.

[18] M. J. M. Christenhusz and J. W. Byng, "The number of known plant species in the world and its annual increase," Phytotaxa. *Magnolia Press* (2016): 261 (3): 201–217.

[19] PlantZAfrica, *Moringa ovalifolia*, http://pza.sanbi.org/moringa-ovalifolia.

[20] Anne Orth Epple, *A Fieldguide to the Plants of Arizona*, Falcon Publishing, Inc. (1995): 134.

[21] PlantZAfrica, *Colophospermum mopane*, http://pza.sanbi.org/colophospermum-mopane.

[22] ———, *Combretum apiculatum,* http://pza.sanbi.org/combretum-apiculatum-subsp-apiculatum.

[23] JSTOR Global Plants, *Rhus pyroides,* https://plants.jstor.org/compilation/Rhus.pyroides.

[24] PlantZAfrica, *Gymnosporia senegalensis,* http://pza.sanbi.org/gymnosporia-senegalensis.

[25] JSTOR Global Plants, *Commiphora glandulosa,* https://plants.jstor.org/compilation/Commiphora.glandulosa.

[26] PlantZAfrica, *Welwitschia mirabilis,* http://pza.sanbi.org/welwitschia-mirabilis.

[27] Botany of Kanna Sceletium Tortuosum, https://www.kanna-sceletium-tortuosum.com/botanical-info/.

[28] Antiquities Act, https://www.doi.gov/ocl/antiquities-act.

[29] iNaturalist, *Bursera graveolens,* https://www.inaturalist.org/taxa/62814-Bursera-graveolens.

[30] ———, *Sesuvium edmonstonei,* https://uk.inaturalist.org/taxa/823572-Sesuvium-edmonstonei; *Sesuvium edmonstonei,* Hook f, Charles Darwin Foundation, https://www.darwinfoundation.org/en/datazone/checklist?species=132.

[31] *"Euphorbia amplexicaulis,"* Plants of the World Online, Retrieved 2 November 2022.

[32] *Croton scouleri* Hook. f., Charles Darwin Foundation, https://www.darwinfoundation.org/en/datazone/checklist?species=1108.

[33] iNaturalist, *Cordia-lutea,* https://www.inaturalist.org/taxa/62830-Cordia-lutea.

[34] ———, *Conocarpus-erectus,* https://www.inaturalist.org/taxa/62850-Conocarpus-erectus.

[35] ———, *Rhizophora-mangle,* https://www.inaturalist.org/taxa/60335-Rhizophora-mangle.

[36] Darwin Lake, https://www.lonelyplanet.com/ecuador/isla-isabela-albemarle/attractions/darwin-lake/a/poi-sig/1298798/1317950; Follow Charles Darwin's Footsteps in the Galapagos Islands, https://www.aquaexpeditions.com/blog/charles-darwin-galapagos-islands.

[37] Britannica: Manchineel, *Hippomane mancinella,* https://www.britannica.com/plant/manchineel.

[38] CABI Digital Library, *Pennisetum purpureum,* https://www.cabidigitallibrary.org/doi/10.1079/cabicompendium.39771.

[39] Missouri Botanical Garden, *Pennisetum setaceum,* https://www.missouribotanicalgarden.org/PlantFinder/PlantFinderDetails.aspx?kempercode=c257.

[40] National Park Service: Invasive Plant Spotlight: Buffelgrass, *Pennisetum ciliare* https://www.nps.gov/articles/spotlight_buffelgrass.htm.

[41] Charles Darwin Foundation, *Darwiniothamnus tenuifolius* (Hook. f.) Harling, https://www.darwinfoundation.org/en/datazone/checklist?species=303.

[42] "Factsheet: *Prosopis juliflora* (prosopis or mesquite)."

[43] "*Parkinsonia aculeata,*" Germplasm Resources Information Network. Agricultural Research Service, United States Department of Agriculture.

[44] Medium Ground Finch, https://animalia.bio/medium-ground-finch.

[45] iNaturalist, *Laguncularia racemose,* https://www.inaturalist.org/taxa/62854-Laguncularia-racemosa.

[46] Darwin Lake, https://www.lonelyplanet.com/ecuador/isla-isabela-albemarle/attractions/darwin-lake/a/poi-sig/1298798/1317950; Follow Charles Darwin's Footsteps in the Galapagos Islands, https://www.aquaexpeditions.com/blog/charles-darwin-galapagos-islands.

[47] ———, *Mollugo flavescens,* https://www.inaturalist.org/taxa/327680-Mollugo-flavescens.

Chapter 5

[1] Claude B. Levenson, *Die Vision des Dalai Lama: Der Friedensnobolpreisträger im Gespräch*, München: Wilhelm Heyne Verlag, 48.

Chapter 6

[1] *Lobelia_deckenii*, https://en.wikipedia.org/wiki/Lobelia_deckenii.

[2] Facts/statistics about ice melting on Mt. Kilimanjaro: Proc Natl Acad Sci U S A. 2009 Nov 24; 106(47): 19770–19775, https://www.ncbi.nlm.nih.gov/pmc/articles/PMC2771743.

[3] PubChem, *Glyphosate*, https://pubchem.ncbi.nlm.nih.gov/compound/glyphosate.

Chapter 7

[1] Gwenda Blair, (October 6, 2015), "How Norman Vincent Peale Taught Donald Trump to Worship Himself," Politico, Arlington, Virginia: Capitol News Company; Norman Vincent Peale, https://www.britannica.com/biography/Norman-Vincent-Peale.

Conclusion

[1] Daniel Yergin, *The New Map: Energy, Climate, and the Clash of Nations*, Penguin Press, New York (2020): 434.